HIGHGATE SCHOOL

HIGHGATE SCHOOL
A History

THOMAS HINDE

ISBN 0 907838 37 8

© Highgate School

First published 1993

Typeset by Action Typesetting Limited, Gloucester

Printed in Great Britain by The Bath Press,
Bath, Avon

Designed by Tom Cabot

Published by James and James (Publishers) Ltd
75 Carleton Road, London N7 0ET

Half-title page: *Highgate Old Chapel. To
the right of the oak is the vault in which
S.T. Coleridge was buried.
His remains were removed to
St Michael's Church in 1961.*

Frontispiece: *Mid-nineteenth century watercolour
showing the bell gate on North Road.*

ACKNOWLEDGEMENTS

I WOULD LIKE TO THANK the many people who have helped me with this history, either by writing to me or by letting me interview them. They include Robert Atkins, Robert Bell, Mrs Geoffrey Bell, Norris Butcher, Alfred Doulton, Ian Davies, Allan Fox, Martin Gilbert, Roy Giles, John Goble, John Gray, William Hallett, Patrick Hughes, Michael Jones, Richard Kennedy, Christine Mead, Patrick Procktor, Christopher Purvis, George Rankine, Robert Read, David Richards, John Rutter, Sushil Shah, Dawson Stewart, Brian Spears, Peter Stone, John Talbot, Thomas Twidell and David Williamson. I am particularly grateful to Sam Eidinow for reading my manuscript and making helpful comments; and to Theodore Mallinson, the school's record keeper, and his assistant, Michael Hammerson. Without their help, encouragement and admirable archive I could not possibly have written what I have.

THOMAS HINDE April 1993

Picture Acknowledgements

The publishers would like to thank the following for permission to reproduce illustrations: London Borough of Camden Local Studies Library, 21, 22, 29, 32, 34, 39, 137; National Portrait Gallery, 16, 30, 139; Highgate Scientific and Literary Institution 35, 57, 67, plate 5; Guildhall Library, Corporation of London, front & rear endpapers, 23, 26, 44, 52, plates 2 & 4; Hulton Deutsch, 139, 140, 141; Skyscan Balloon Photography, plate 8; cartoons by Gerard Hoffnung on pages 106–7 are the copyright of Annetta Hoffnung and reproduced by her kind permission; Brian Weeks, 125; Simon Walker, 135; Michael Morelle, back jacket illustration.

The old Dyne House, demolished in 1966, shown here in the Illustrated London News, *1959. Boys can be seen emerging from the back entrance that led to the 'Tuck Shop'.*

CONTENTS

	Acknowledgements	*5*
1	The Founder and his School	*9*
2	The School and the Village	*19*
3	Dr Owen Goes to Law	*33*
4	Dr Dyne – Second Founder	*45*
5	Succeeding an Institution	*61*
6	Allcock – Dear Old Boy	*71*
7	An Aeroplane on the Roof – Johnston Elevates Science	*81*
8	Another War	*99*
9	Doulton Spans the 1960s	*113*
10	Calm and Care	*123*
11	Today and Tomorrow	*131*
	Selected List of Old Cholmeleians	*137*
	Index	*142*

Edmund Grindal, Bishop of London, donated Highgate chapel and two acres of land to Sir Roger Cholmeley in April 1565.

THE FOUNDER AND HIS SCHOOL
1562–1583

THE DISSOLUTION OF the monasteries by Henry VIII between 1536 and 1541 is one of the best known events of English history. Less well known is the fact that their demise, together with the abolition of the country's chantries in 1547, demolished the English educational system as it had grown up through the previous five centuries. All over the country schools run by the Roman Catholic Church were closed to be replaced by schools devoted to the new Protestant faith.

At first this process was comparatively gradual. In Henry's remaining years some sixty new grammar schools were founded, including eleven cathedral schools, and a further fifteen in the brief reign of his son Edward VI, and it was only after the interlude of Mary's five years, when it seemed as if the whole process might be reversed, that this sluggish flow became a torrent. By 1577 the Revd William Harrison could write in his *Description of England* 'there are not many corporate towns now under the Queen's dominion that do not have one grammar school at least'. He put the total at 350, but the full number founded in Tudor times has been estimated at nearer 800. Among them were many which were to become famous: Rugby, Harrow, Uppingham, Felsted and Merchant Taylors' for example. Among them, too, was 'the free Grammar School of Sir Roger Cholmeley, Knight', at Highgate.

Today Highgate School possesses, as one of its most interesting records, a heavy leather-bound volume in which its first Governors kept their minutes. Its opening page records that the building of the school's chapel and schoolhouse began on 3 July 1576 and finished in September 1578. These dates are supported by a receipt from the Bishop of London dated the previous January for money received for wood to burn the bricks for the new buildings. But by the time they were finished it was no less than thirteen years since the date of the official founding of the school in 1565.

A detail from the original Governors' minute book showing the shield of Sir Roger Cholmeley.

That was also the year in which Sir Roger Cholmeley, the founder, had died. He had been one of those lawyers who had thrived on the mass of litigation which resulted from the religious controversies of the time and the redistribution of the old Church's properties. He was the son of Sir Richard Cholmeley of Golston, Yorkshire, Lieutenant of the Tower of London, but because he was illegitimate was not left the family's Yorkshire estates. He did, however, inherit valuable property in and around London, including some in Highgate, and he subsequently acquired more there. Eventually he came to live in the High Street in a house on the site of today's Fairseat.

Meanwhile he had prospered in his career. In 1509 he was readmitted to Lincoln's Inn (neither his date of birth nor the date when he was first admitted are known). In 1524 he was called to the bench, in 1537 he was knighted and during the rest of Henry VIII's reign he held various important legal positions including that of Recorder of London for ten years (1535–45) and Chief Baron of Exchequer (1545–6).

Under Edward VI he rose in 1552 to his highest position as Lord Chief Justice of the King's Bench. Unwisely, however, he witnessed the will of the young and frail king, intended to make Lady Jane Grey rather than the princesses Mary or Elizabeth, his successor. When, despite the will, Mary became queen, she sent Cholmeley to the Tower.

He was heavily fined, but was released after six weeks and to an extent restored to favour. He took part in the notorious trial of Sir Nicholas Throckmorton (accused of having been involved in the Wyatt rebellion of 1554). The jury acquitted Throckmorton, but the judges attempted to force them to reverse their verdict and when they refused fined them £1,000 for contempt. Cholmeley was not only party to this bullying, but declared that he would have Throckmorton convicted on some other charge. Perhaps he was hoping to be restored by Mary to his old position but if so his plan failed and though he was made a Privy Councillor and was MP for Middlesex until 1559, he eventually retired to Highgate. His true sympathies were probably always Protestant, and Princess Elizabeth, on her way from Ashridge to London – also to be questioned about complicity in Wyatt's rising – stayed the night of 15 February 1555 with the Cholmeleys at Highgate.

If these were the main events of Cholmeley's public life, and were fairly typical of a successful lawyer of the time, his private life and character are more intriguing. *The Black Book* of Lincoln's Inn records a succession of his offences and punishments. In 1513 he was fined 3s. 4d. for failing to attend a lecture ('bycase he loste one mote'); in 1517 when Christmas Butler he was fined 10s. for 'exercising bad government in the Inn ... in breaking the doors of chambers', and for spending too much on Christmas wine; in 1518 he was fined 6s. 8d. as Senior Barrister, for failing to prevent the chaplain and others playing cards and dicing in chambers; in 1523 he was fined 3s. 4d. for dicing during the Lent vacation; and in 1528 he was threatened with expulsion unless he paid the lately retired steward a debt for 'reposts and commons'.

Cholmeley's rackety youth was apparently well known. When, many years later, a group of young men was brought before him to be disciplined, one of them reminded him that he had once been 'a good fellow'. By then Cholmeley had become respectable, and replied, 'Indeed, in youth I was, as you are now; and I had twelve fellows like unto myself, but not one of them came unto a good end. And therefore, follow not my example in youth, but follow my counsel in age; lest you meet either with poverty or Tyburn in the way.'

Cholmeley had probably become interested in education when he had been one of the Royal Commissioners responsible for seeing that the confiscated possessions of chantries were put to good and godly use, this to include the founding of grammar schools. It was understandable that he should found such a school himself in the place to which he had retired. Highgate at the time was a hamlet, set in the country, but comparatively easily reached from the City, with the result that a number of prosperous merchants, lawyers and other professional men had either settled or acquired country houses there. It was an ideal place for one of the richest of them, now an old man of about 70, to make a gesture which would promote the new faith and win him credit in heaven.

The official date of his foundation, 1565, is well documented. On 29 January that year he obtained letters patent from the queen allowing his foundation. The Latin document required it to be a school 'for the education, institution and instruction of Boys and Youths in Grammar'. It added, in a phrase which was to affect the school for the next two and a half centuries, that it should also make provision 'in some convenient manner for the Relief and Support of certain poor persons dwelling within the said Town or Hamlet of Highgate'.

Just over two months later (6 April) Cholmeley obtained a second grant of letters patent. This confirmed the earlier one but contained new provisions, most importantly naming six Governors for the school and requiring them to draw

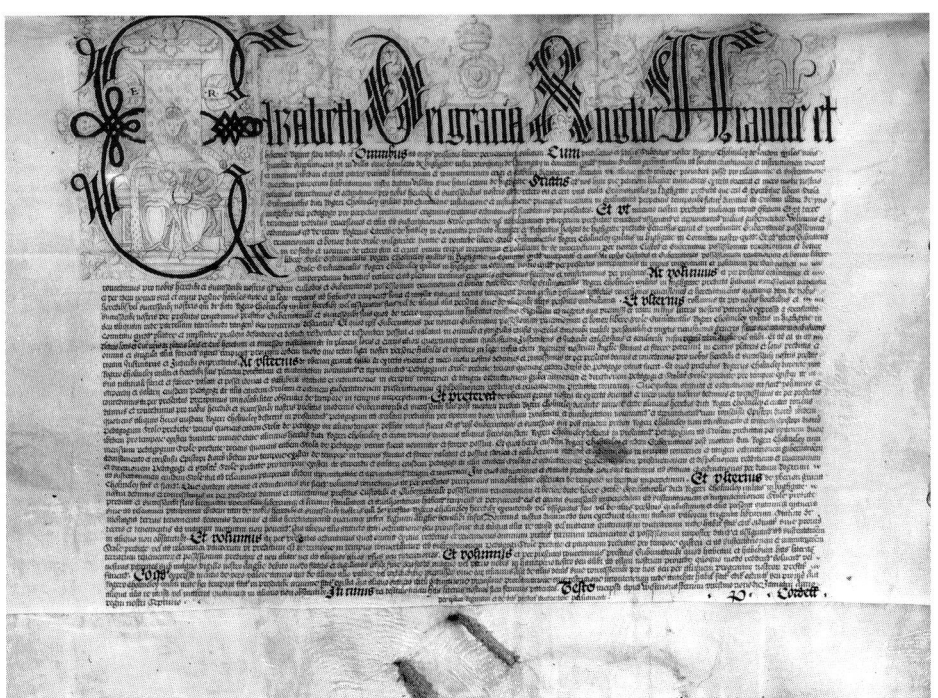

The letters patent of Queen Elizabeth I, 6 April 1565, authorising the foundation of the school and nominating Governors.

Above: *Grant of the chapel and two acres of land by Edmund Grindal, Bishop of London, 27 April 1565.*

Above right: *Shortly after the Bishop of London's donation to Sir Roger Cholmeley he formally handed the property over to the school foundation with this grant, 7 June 1565.*

up statutes and appoint a learned man to be its Master. Cholmeley's desire to hand over his school to Governors and the fact that one of them was his nephew, Jasper Cholmeley, suggest that he already knew he was terminally ill.

Before he died he brought the school a more important benefit. Like the grant of permission from the queen, this was arranged in two stages. First came the gift on 27 April to Cholmeley of a chapel and two acres of land at Highgate by Edmund Grindal, Bishop of London. Bishop Grindal was even more strongly associated with Protestantism than Cholmeley. While Cholmeley had stayed and compromised, Grindal had spent Mary's reign abroad. Clearly, however, he now accepted Cholmeley as a fellow reformer and was glad to support a school where boys would be educated in the new faith; indeed, he founded a grammar school himself at St Bees in the Lake District, his birthplace.

It was in his power to make the gift because the chapel lay in the manor of Haringey, of which the Bishop of London had been the Lord since the Norman Conquest. The chapel had belonged to a hermitage since at least 1364, when William Phelippe was named as the hermit in a royal grant. The names of several subsequent hermits are known and one of them (unnamed) is said to have built the causeway over swampy ground which first connected Highgate with Islington. Their chapel stood close to Highgate Hill which by Tudor times had become the most important of Highgate's roads, since it formed part of the route from London to the north. The toll-gate here, which was the third entrance to the Bishop of London's park of Haringey and which gave Highgate its name, is still commemorated in the name of the Gate House. The chapel's central position would certainly have made it convenient for the inhabitants of the hamlet, whose parish churches were several miles away at St Pancras or Hornsey, but whether or not it had, as a result, become a 'chapel of ease' is far from certain.

True, the sixteenth-century surveyor, John Norden, wrote about St Pancras church that it 'was now and then visited with Kentish Town and Highgate, which are members thereof; but they seldom come there, for they have chapels of ease within themselves.' But Norden, writing in 1596, may have been referring to a time after the founding of the school. The records of the Star Chamber Court are more suggestive. On 23 May 1503 the Vicar of St Pancras and a party were beating of his parish when they came into conflict with Thomas Walterkyn, the hermit of the time.

> According to the hermit, when he was in the garden with his servant they came into his house, broke down the paling of his orchard and garden, hit him over the arm with a bill, and would have murdered him if he had not escaped to the steeple of the hermitage, where he remained until they had gone. He also alleged that they stole two altar cloths, a surplice and a 'grayle', i.e. a book of antiphons. The Vicar replied that they were going in procession as usual about their parish when the hermit would not allow them to pass, although courteously asked to do so. The hermit was in his garden, armed with a great club, and having with him two others also armed with clubs, they suddenly struck William Chadwick, of St Pancras, yeoman, over the pale. They broke some of the pales and then the St Pancras people pulled down some more to make room to pass.

Far from having stolen the grayle, the Vicar continued, the hermit, who was a man 'of ill conversation and rule', had pawned it. A grayle is indeed a book with responses, suitable for use with a congregation; if the hermit possessed one, was he conducting services for the locals? And was the Vicar 'going in procession as usual', or was he engaged in some attempt to suppress the hermit's activities? But the story is hardly conclusive and even if Lord Chancellor Eldon had known it when he delivered his famous judgment of 1827 and declared that the chapel had *not* been a chapel of ease, he would probably have reached the same conclusion.

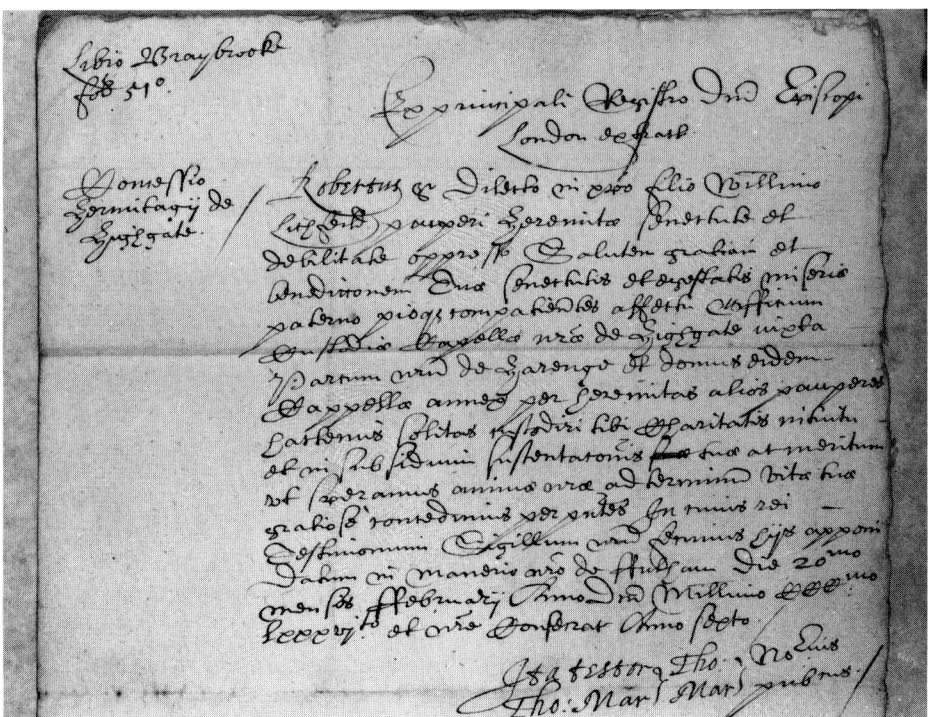

Endowment by the Bishop of London to Sir Roger Cholmeley of Highgate chapel and two acres of land on Highgate Common (still occupied by the School), 27 April 1565.

A sixteenth century copy of an original grant of Highgate chapel to a hermit in 1364 by the Bishop of London, who as Lord of the Manor of Haringey since Norman times had control over the chapel.

The second stage by which the school acquired the chapel and land was duly completed on 7 June 1565 when Cholmeley handed them over, together with an endowment of London properties worth £10. 3s. 4d. a year. Perhaps he considered that he had done enough for the school. When he died later that month (he was buried on 2 July 1565, at St Martin's, Ludgate, where his grave disappeared when the church was destroyed in the Great Fire of London) his will made the school no further bequests.

It did, however, leave £5 to 'Simon of Heygate ... towards his finding to schole', and it was once suggested that Simon was the Master of the school. But since the bequest was sandwiched between one of £3 and a black coat to Cholmeley's cook and another of £5 and a black gown to his maiden servant, it seems more likely that Simon was a member of his household, and the money was to help him get an education at some unspecified place.

If the school was firmly established with land and Governors by mid-1565, what, it may be asked, were these Governors doing between then and starting to build the brick chapel and schoolhouse in 1576? They were men of wealth and influence, all six likely to support the school, either because they had Highgate connections, or because they were sympathisers with the cause of religious reform. First named was Sir William Hewett, with an income from his estates of £6,000 a year and a country house at Highgate. He, too, had countersigned the will of Edward VI which had got Cholmeley into trouble with Queen Mary. He had been a Master of the Clothiers' Company and Lord Mayor of London. Others were Sir Roger Marten, to be Lord Mayor of London in 1567, who had a brother with Highgate property, and Richard Hodges, who had bought from Cholmeley the land to the south of the High Street on which Bisham House subsequently stood. As for Cholmeley's nephew, Jasper, he too was a rich Highgate resident, once he had inherited most of his uncle's properties.

They (and their replacements, since some died soon) had not been idle. Though the brick chapel and schoolhouse of 1576–8 are the earliest recorded school buildings, they were not the first, for a carpenter's plan of 1575 shows what they replaced. A schoolhouse 32 feet long and 12 feet broad had stood probably on the site of today's North Road quadrangle. South of this, attached at right angles to form an L, stood a chapel, 50 ft. long and 24 ft. broad. The plan shows sites to which each of these buildings were to be moved, presumably when the new chapel and schoolhouse were built. Since they were movable, and since the plan was a carpenter's and because of their lengths (the schoolhouse of two 16-ft. bays, the chapel of roughly three bays) they were undoubtedly timber-framed. Here then was a chapel far larger than a hermit would have needed – and here was a largish pre-1576 schoolhouse.

A clue to the date at least of the schoolhouse perhaps once existed in a stone inscription fixed to the west end of the brick chapel:

Anno Dmni 1562, Sir Roger Cholmley, knt: Ld Cheife Barron of ye Exchequer And after that Ld Cheife Justice of the King's Bench Did Institute and Erect at his owne charges This publique and Free Gramer Schoole and Provided the same to be established and confirmed By The

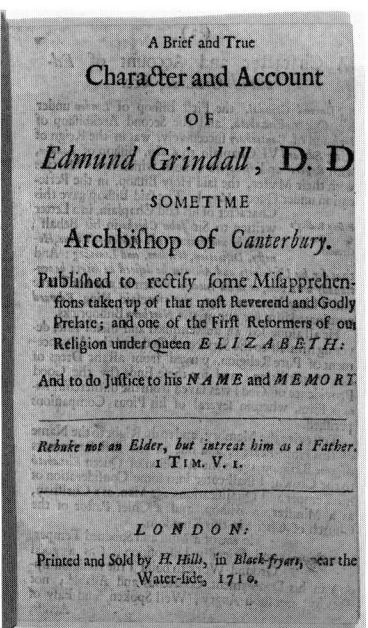

In common with many powerful religious figures in the late seventeenth century the fortunes of Grindal (the more usual spelling), later Archbishop of Canterbury, varied. This 1710 booklet was a posthumous defence of his name.

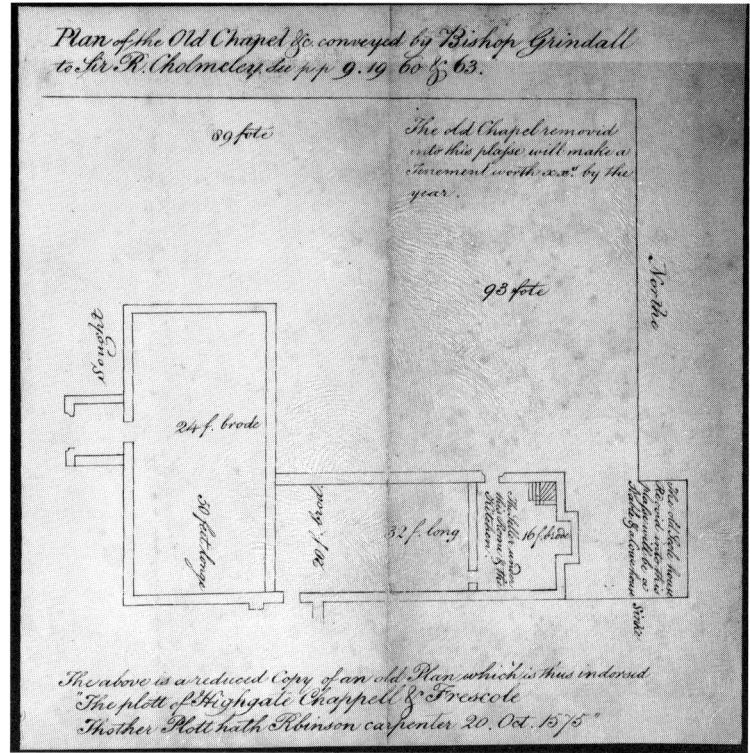

Above left: *An 1840s copy of a plan of the schoolhouse and chapel before rebuilding work in 1575.*

Above: *The west end of the 1575 brick chapel (from an 1805 print) showing the stone inscription.*

Letters Patent of Queene Elizabeth. Hee endowinge the same with yearely Maynetaynance – which Schoole Edwyn Sandys Bishop of London Enlarged ANo DNI 1565 – By the addition of This Chappel for Divine Service, and By other Endowments of Piete and Devotion; Since which the said Chappel Hath been Enlarged By the Pietie and Bounty of Divers Honble and Worthy Personages.

As this inscription refers to an enlargement of the chapel, it was clearly placed there after the first enlargement of 1616, and it contained a serious inaccuracy. Either the date, 1565, was wrong, or the bishop's name, Sandys, was wrong, because in 1565 Grindal was Bishop of London. It does not follow that the date, 1562, for the institution and erection of the school is a mistake. There would almost certainly have been negotiations before the issue of the legal documents of 1565, and it is possible that Cholmeley and Grindal had already come to some informal arrangement which allowed Cholmeley to occupy the land, even perhaps to build the timber-framed chapel and schoolhouse. Whoever devised the inscription may have known of some tradition or document now lost which confirmed this. The date 1562 was certainly accepted by Domville, one of the pamphleteers of the 1820s, who wrote, 'it may be assumed that the school was in fact instituted in 1562, though it was not confirmed by letters patent till three years afterwards'. And Lord Chancellor Eldon agreed that it was 'in or about the year one thousand five hundred and sixty-two' that Cholmeley had instituted his school, subsequently applying for the letters patent, granted in 1565.

Whatever the date of the first school buildings, it can hardly be a coincidence

Bishop Edwin Sandys and his wife. Sandys followed Grindal as Bishop of London and quickly became closely involved with the school.

that the arrival in 1570 of a new Bishop of London, Edwin Sandys, was quickly followed in December 1571 by the issue of the first school statutes. Sandys, like Cholmeley, had supported Lady Jane Grey's claim to the throne during Edward VI's reign and been subsequently imprisoned in the Tower by Mary, but on his release, like Grindal, had escaped abroad and not returned until Mary had died and Elizabeth become queen. He was, according to the *Dictionary of National Biography*, 'an obstinate and conscientious puritan'. More interestingly from the school's point of view, he was a scholar – one of the translators of the Bishops' Bible of 1565 – and, like Grindal, had founded a grammar school at his birthplace, Hawkshead, in the Lake District.

Clearly Sandys took considerable interest in the Highgate school, for the statutes, which the Governors issued on 14 December 1571, were not only signed by him, but specifically said in their preamble to have required 'the assent of the Right Reverend Father in God the Lord Bishop of London'. They gave much emphasis to the part which religion should play in the life of the school. The first item which the boys were to learn was their ABC. This was a small book originally produced in Henry VIII's time, which began with the alphabet, set out in different scripts, but for the most part consisted of the Ten

Commandments, of graces to be said at different meals, and of a long catechism of questions and answers. In one edition (the school has several in its archives) this began:

> These questions the master ought to demaunde and to lerne his scolers.
> 'Speke my good chyld. Tel me what art thou.' The chyld anunswereth.
> 'As concernynge my first byrth, I am a creature of God endowed with wyt and reason, the son of Adam. And as touching my newe and seconde byrth, I knowlege my selfe to be a Chrystian.'

Another edition ended:

> This little catechisme learned
> By heart, (for so it ought,)
> The Primer [Prayer Book] next commanded is
> For children to be taught.

The boys of Highgate were also to be instructed in 'other English books' and in writing, but only in grammar (Latin and Greek) when 'they shall grow ripe thereto'.

The school day was to begin at 7 a.m. with prayers, the boys 'devoutly kneeling down on their knees' and after a lunch break from 11 a.m. to 1 p.m. to end at 5 p.m. (6 p.m. in summer) with more prayers. These were to be conducted by the school's Master who was to be a 'graduate of good Life and honest Conversation and no light person'. More significantly, he was to conduct a range of services in 'ye chappel of Highgate next adjoyning ye ffree school', listed as morning and evening services on Sundays and holidays, evening prayers on Wednesdays, morning prayers on Fridays and evening prayers on Saturdays and the eves of all holy days. The only service he was excused was morning prayers on the first Sunday of each month when the locals were required to go to 'their several parish churches' to take communion. The school's statutes thus make it clear that these services were for the people of Highgate, and whatever the chapel may have been in earlier times they describe it as a 'chapel of ease'.

The Master was to perform these religious duties and his teaching duties without the help of a second master (usually called an Usher) for an annual salary of £10, which he could only supplement by charging each new pupil 4 pence (and by cutting eight loads of firewood a year from the Bishop of London's woods). By comparison the master of the King's School, Canterbury, a school founded twenty-five years before Highgate, with fifty scholars (only a few more than Highgate's forty) received £20 a year and his usher £10. Highgate's boys were to come from Highgate, Holloway, Haringey, Finchley or Kentish Town, but also from 'Towns thereto adjoyning' if these places could not provide enough. Finally the statutes appointed Johnson Charle to be the school's Master.

The total cost of the 1576–8 buildings was, according to Norden, £490, of which £150 came from the grant of new leases on the school's properties, £49 from Jasper Cholmeley and £291 from other contributors including £172 from Bishop Sandys and William Cordell. After Cholmeley, Sir William Cordell was the school's most generous early benefactor. He had had many connections with

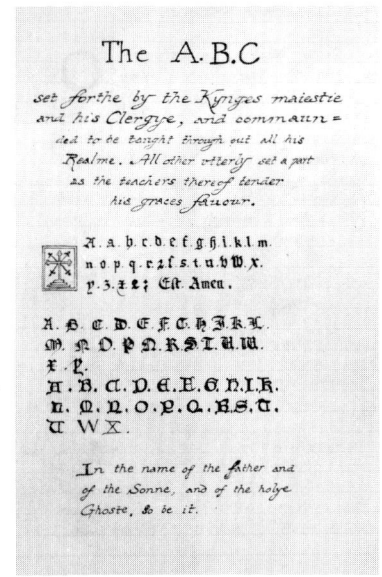

An 1871 copy of the ABC, a catechism and letter book which would have been the main schoolbook in the late sixteenth century.

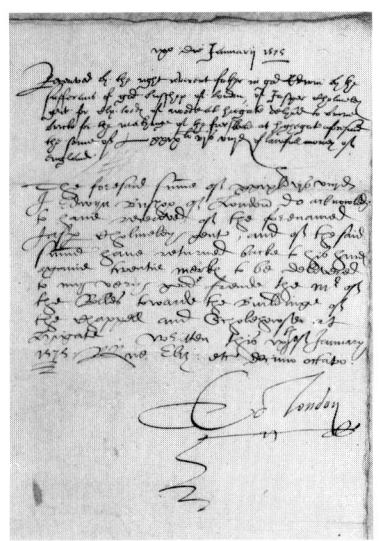

Bishop of London's receipt for payment for wood to fire bricks for building of school, 9 January 1575.

Cholmeley, belonging also to Lincoln's Inn, of which he became a Bencher. In 1537 he had succeeded Cholmeley as Recorder of London. He, too, had compromised with Mary, and was her Solicitor General when Wyatt was tried for treason. During her reign he became Master of the Rolls and Speaker of the House of Commons. He was connected with the founding of both Merchant Taylors' School and St John's College, Cambridge, and in 1576 he became a Governor of Highgate School.

A strange legal tangle now occurred. In March 1578 (new style) the queen granted to a 'gentleman pensioner', John Farnham, 'our little ruinous cottage Chapel or hermitage with its appurts lying and being in Highgate'. Though the Chantries Act (1547) had appropriated to the Crown most colleges, chapels and chantries, some had escaped and some had not yet been disposed of. At the same time the queen granted Farnham other chapels in Kent, Shropshire, Somerset and the city of York.

The grant is surprising, to say the least. By March 1578 the new chapel, presumably replacing the previous one, had been under construction for some eighteen months. The fact that no land was attached to the Highgate grant, as it was to Farnham's other grants, suggests one possible explanation: that the old chapel did exist, the earliest one (not the timber-framed one of the carpenter's plan) never having been demolished but still standing as a ruin in some corner of the school's two acres. More probably Farnham (and the queen's lawyers) assumed that the chapel, like most others, had been annexed to the Crown and did not know of the Bishop of London's right to grant it to Cholmeley.

Farnham seems to have realised that there had been a mistake. Five years later, he 'sold' the chapel to Roger Puleston, the Receiver General of the school, who, the following year 're-leased' it to the school. Though the Governors accepted this arrangement they recorded in their minute book that 'They did not hold by virtue of these documents [Puleston's re-lease etc.] but by virtue of letters patent of Elizabeth, 1565 – but for avoiding all disputes into which they might be driven in defence of the said chapel, they accepted this release.'

By then Johnson Charle had been succeeded by another Master, Edward Smythe, about whom equally little is known. Nevertheless, the school, now firmly established with statutes, schoolhouse and chapel, seemed as well set to survive and prosper as any of the numerous grammar schools founded in the fifty years after the Reformation. Only gradually did its disadvantages become clear, disadvantages which these early events had compounded.

THE SCHOOL AND THE VILLAGE
1584–1790

Survive Cholmeley's free grammar school did, but it did not prosper. Its decline has been explained in several ways. Since it was not a well-endowed school and could only afford the poor salary of £10 for its Master, a succession of undistinguished men held the position. In 1594 the Master, Joshua Williams, was removed for neglecting his duties. Schools of the time which acquired a good reputation almost always did so because of the exceptional qualities of a particular Master. A few middle-class boys attended Highgate School – one of them Jasper Cholmeley's son, Hugh – and this might suggest that Latin and Greek were taught, but it seems unlikely that this was the general practice or that many pupils benefited, since they were more and more often referred to as 'poor boys'.

Highgate also had a better endowed rival, the grammar school of Harrow, only a few miles away. And though Highgate village had a number of prosperous residents, it was still a comparatively small place, lacking a group of middle-class parents who, if they used the school, might have insisted on better masters.

But the school's failure to prosper probably had a more fundamental cause: the remoteness of Highgate from its two parish churches. The school's statutes, no doubt as a consequence and without recognising where it might lead, accepted that the chapel was for village as well as school. It was this connection between the chapel and the village community which most seriously harmed the school.

Step by step the chapel and its functions grew in importance, and at the same time so did the villagers' expectations of it. In 1616 and again in 1628 it was enlarged by public subscription. From 1617 it was licensed for the performance of marriages, and at the same time villagers began to be buried in its yard and to have monuments to their memories erected inside. The monument to William Platt, probably one of the earliest, can still be seen in St Pancras parish church, to which it was moved in 1833.

Meanwhile in 1615 the villagers complained that the Master's reading of the services was inaudible, and their dissatisfaction must have continued because at some time during the next twenty-two years they secured a preacher to come periodically and preach them a more satisfactory sermon. When William Platt died in 1637 he left £10 a year to the chapel's preacher, and 20 shillings for each sermon he preached.

These sermons were almost certainly Puritan in tone, for Highgate was predominantly a Puritan village. The Governors of the school were also for the most part Puritan, and managed to have one Royalist governor, Sir Thomas Gardiner, removed. In 1644 they were also probably responsible for having the school's Master, Dr Thomas Carter, removed and imprisoned for fifteen months, allegedly for drunkenness. The evidence against him, however, included a claim

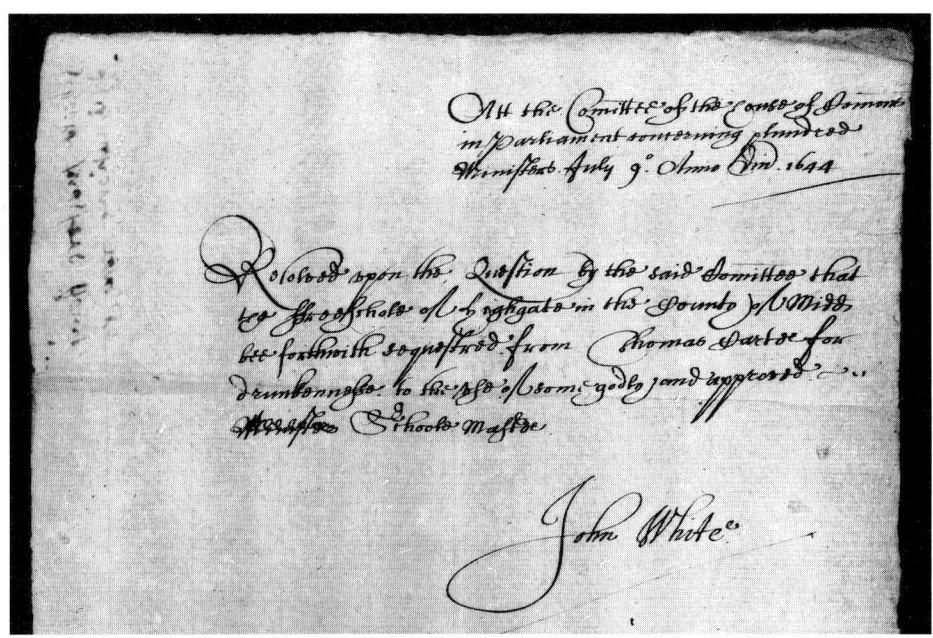

The removal of the Head Master, Dr Carter, by Parliamentary Committee 'for drunkenness', 1644.

that he had said 'they were mad that would read Commons' order on innovations'; and Carter himself claimed that his offence had been his continuing to read services from the Book of Common Prayer. The Governors were not especially successful at replacing him, four Masters coming and going before the Restoration.

Most powerful of these Puritans was Sir John Wollaston, Governor of the school from 1630 until his death in 1658, a prosperous London goldsmith, Lord Mayor in 1644. Like Platt, he provided £10 a year for the chapel's preacher. He also built the original six almshouses in Southwood Lane for the poor of Highgate and when he died appointed the school's Governors to manage them. This new responsibility helped to transform the Governors from school managers into a body more in the nature of a parish council.

Another Parliamentarian and Lord Mayor to become a Governor was John Ireton, brother of General Henry Ireton. John was knighted by Cromwell, but after the Restoration he was excluded from the Act of Indemnity and sent to the Tower. Two years later, when he became ill, he was exiled to the Scillies. Since he could not visit Highgate, the remaining Governors asked the Recorder of London whether they might replace him, but received the reply that although Ireton could not attend meetings without committing a legal offence, he remained a Governor. As a result, until Ireton died in 1689 the school in practice had five Governors.

The Restoration of Charles II, however, led also to the restoration of Dr Carter, who continued to be Master until 1670. During these and the following years there is again conflicting evidence about the nature of the school. On the one hand a boy named W. Godwin, who became a student at St John's College, Cambridge, in 1668, was 'bred at Highgate under Mr Carter 2 years'. The verb 'bred' may suggest that he was an early boarder rather than one of the school's free scholars, but his entry to St John's shows that Carter was to some extent teaching the classics. This is supported by a list of books in the school's library in 1673, which included Greek and Latin dictionaries and works by Caesar and Cicero. Two of Carter's successors, Robert Pierce of Trinity College, Oxford, and Thomas Brown of Christ's College, Cambridge, must have taught the most distinguished Cholmeleian so far, Nicholas Rowe, a pupil until he was fifteen in 1688. Rowe's best-known work was a life of Shakespeare and edition of his works. George I appointed him Poet Laureate, and when he died in 1718 he was buried in Westminster Abbey's Poets' Corner.

Between Carter's departure and the end of the century, the school's Masters continued to be graduates, as the statutes required, eight out of ten from Oxford. Furthermore, in 1670 the Governors' minute book makes first mention of an Usher at the school. On the other hand it also records that Robert King, one of those apparently well-educated Masters, was merely required when appointed in 1677 to 'instruct ye free scholars in reading of English and writing and in English Grammar'. And four years earlier complaints were received about another of them, Ellis Price of Brasenose College, Oxford, for begetting 'a Bastard Child' by one Isabela Briggs. Ellis had promised to marry Isabela, but Isabela now found that he had married another woman. The Governors ordered that he be 'displaced and ousted of his School-master-Shipp'. During the second half of the seventeenth century the education which the boys of Highgate School received must have been as various as the characters of its Masters.

In 1712 the Governors chose for the new Master the Revd John Browne. About Browne more can be said than about his predecessors. The bond he signed on 25 February required him to instruct the school's forty scholars 'according to the direction of the Founder' and not to 'employ any of the said free Boys in going of errands or any other business whereby to hinder ... them in their learning'. It added that he was not to keep more than ten 'wardens' in his house. Nor was he to let any part of the schoolhouse, a repetition of an order of 1711, suggesting that this had been a practice of past Masters. Two years later he was allowed an additional five boarders, and the Governors awarded him £10 for having been 'diligent in instructing the poore Boyes'. From the start Browne seems to have

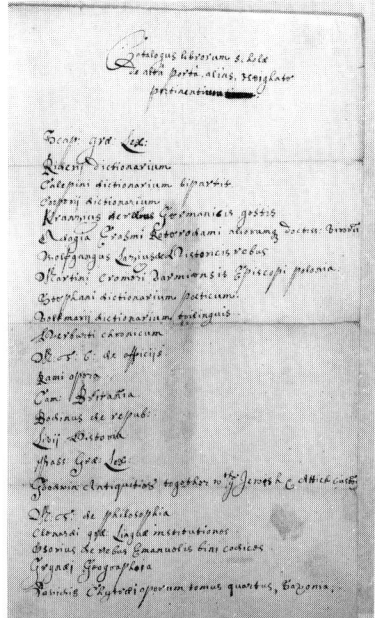

List of books found at the school by the new Head Master John Seeley, 1673 — including Camden's Britannia *and works by Caesar, Cicero, Erasmus and Livy.*

Nicholas Rowe, pupil in the 1680s and Poet Laureate under George I.

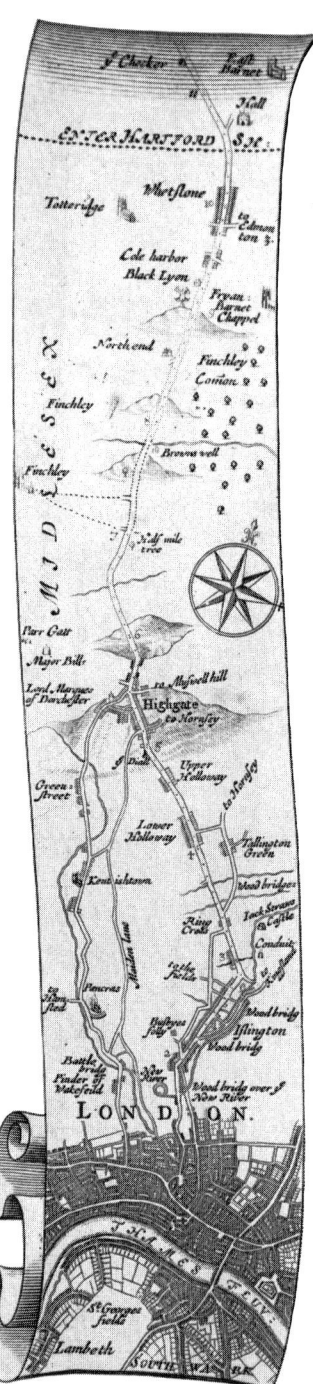

This late seventeenth century route map shows the importance of Highgate Hill as the main road north from the City of London.

taken his duties seriously; two months before he signed his bond he copied out in full the school's 1571 statutes.

How involved he was, however, in the three most important developments of his time – the founding of a girls' school, the enlarging of the chapel and the rebuilding of the almshouses – is less certain, and the fact that his name does not appear among the seventy-one subscribers to the chapel's enlargement is perhaps significant.

The girls are first heard of on 2 May 1719 when the Governors petitioned the Bishop of London for help with the erecting of a school building for them and a house for their Mistress. Their school had 'lately' been started, the Governors explained, and was instructing its twenty-four girls in 'the Principles of our Religion, as they are contained in the most excellent Catechism of our Church, which they are made to rehearse at appointed times, as well as the Boys, before the Congregation; they are likewise taught to read and work and are cloathed once a year'.

The petition was presented to the Bishop by Edward Pauncefort, the prosperous owner of Lauderdale House, who had become a Governor in 1711, but the Bishop's response is not known. The next entry in the Governor's minute book is his licence, dated 6 October 1719, to enlarge the chapel. Precise details are given, with a plan, and the list of donors follows. The Bishop himself contributed a modest £20, and the total raised – £261. 7s. 6d. – proved far from adequate, the balance of £700. 6s. 6d. being given by Pauncefort. But the work was done quickly, and precisely a year later the Bishop consecrated the new part of the chapel.

That was not the end of Pauncefort's generosity. In March 1721 an agreement was signed for the rebuilding of the almshouses and the inclusion of a schoolroom for the girls and rooms above for their Mistress. All was completed the following year, according to the plaque which can still be seen above the main entrance:

> Anno 1722
> The six Almes-Houses found by
> SR JOHN WOOLASTON Knt.
> Being very old, and decayed were
> pull'd down and These twelve built in
> their Room: together with a School House
> for the Charity Girls, at the Sole Charge of
> EDWARD PAUNCEFORT Esq.
> One of the Governours and Treasurer of the
> Chappell and Free-School of HIGHGATE

Though the Bishop of London gave the ground for the almshouses, they cost Pauncefort a further £373, and on 2 October 1723 he was formally thanked by the Governors for his 'very ... Generous Benefaction'.

To complete the story of the girls' school, it survived until about 1843 when it was absorbed into St Michael's School. The almshouses remained connected with the school for far longer, only being handed over to Hornsey Churches Housing Association in 1980. Throughout this time they were a recurring

The Wollaston and Pauncefort almshouses, Southwood Lane, rebuilt 1722. From an 1877 watercolour.

preoccupation. Typically, on 22 January 1736, the Governors ordered 'that Mary Nicholls by reason of her Scandalous way of life and Misbehaviour and by burning the shutters of her Windows and otherwise endangering the Almshouses be discharged out of the Almshouse she is in possession of and that if she deliver up the Key she be paid the £2 10 0 due the 4th Instant and if she refuses so to do that a new Lock and Key be put on the door.'

By now the Governors were accepting gifts, not to the charity in general, but for specific purposes. These had already included a new clock and surplice ('the old ones being decayed and worne out') and, again from Pauncefort, 'all the Plate belonging to the Communion Table double guilt'. After the chapel's rebuilding, Lady Child gave 'Two large fine Common prayer Books with Covers of Crimson Velvet, with gold Letters, fringe etc.', Lady Rebecca Moyer 'A Velvet Cover bound about with gold Lace' and Mr Schoppens 'A very fine Damask Linnen cloth for the Communion Table'. In 1752 Samuel Foster left £300 for the support of widows in the almshouses.

With the chapel enlarged to something like a parish church, the Governors began to charge rent for thirty-two of its double pews. At the same time (October 1723) they ordered a series of annual payments to its officers. The

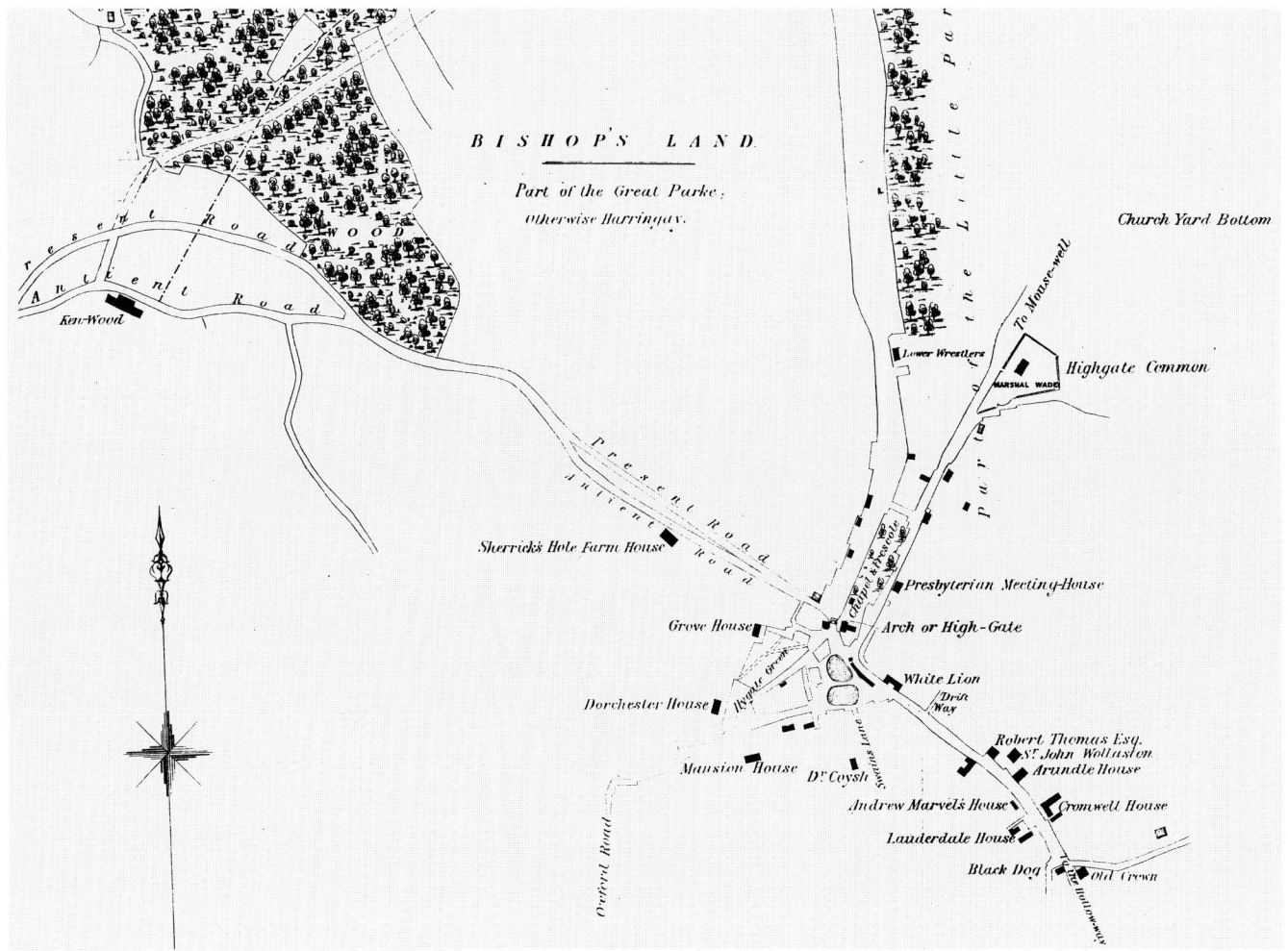

A map (drawn in the nineteenth century) showing Highgate in the early eighteenth century.

Preacher was to receive £50 (next month increased to £60), the organist £20, the clerk £4 plus £1 for winding the clock, the glazier £2 and the clock-repairer £1. The Preacher, Dr Lewis Atterbury, was granted the pews to the west of the pulpit free of rent.

Atterbury additionally benefited from Platt's and Wollaston's bequests of £10 a year each, not to mention the stipends of the parishes of Hornsey and Shepperton-on-Thames. Against this, the salary of Browne, the Master, and of the Revd Thomas Horton who succeeded him in 1728, was £20 a year. Even after 1726, when they received an additional £10 annually from a Pauncefort bequest their income was a mere £30, whereas the Preacher's, from Highgate sources alone, was almost three times as large. It is hardly surprising that Horton and Atterbury quarrelled.

In March 1729 (new style) Horton claimed that he was being deprived of various chapel dues by Atterbury, who had sent him 'three briefs' demanding the monies of the chapel collections. Horton told the Governors that he knew of no case in which a person got paid for a service which it was the duty of someone else to perform. On another occasion, when Horton had churched a wife and baptised her child at no charge, the clerk of the chapel had collected one shilling and sixpence from the father on behalf of himself and the Preacher. At a recent burial a certain Mr Edward Yardley, a clergyman occasionally employed by the Preacher in the chapel, had insisted on performing the service, which Horton had only allowed him to do 'to prevent the raising of a disturbance, wherewith the said Yardley threatened him, at so improper a time'.

More significantly, Horton had discovered that a list of bequests to the charity drawn up in 1697 had had the words 'Preacher' or 'Lecturer' changed in every case to 'Minister' when reissued in 1725. At the top of the earlier list a note claims that the changes to the second list were made by Atterbury. Clearly Atterbury was trying to establish the Preacher rather than the school's Master as the parson of the 'parish' of Highgate, and the Governors were presumably not objecting. There is no evidence that at this time they thought that they might be behaving improperly. In 1711 they discovered that none of them knew the whereabouts of the chest in which their documents should be kept, nor could remember whether it had ever existed, but they expressed no anxiety about the contents of the documents. By the time Atterbury had died in 1731 and been succeeded by Yardley they had imposed a compromise. The Master was to perform baptisms, marriages and burials at the chapel, but Master and Preacher were to 'administer the sacrament of the Lord's Supper alternately'.

Soon the Governors were busying themselves with matters which were related neither to school, chapel nor almshouses. In 1731 they agreed to build a brick shed in the chapel yard for a village fire-engine. Two fire-engines were bought, together with several pipes and buckets, by a public subscription, a third of

THE Inhabitants of the Hamlet of *HIGHGATE*, in the County of *Middlesex*, being desirous, as far as in them lies, to prevent any Robberies or Felonies being committed in the said Hamlet for the future, have enter'd into a voluntary Subscription for a Reward for the Discovery of such Robberies or Felonies, and therefore they have paid into the Hands of *JOHN EDWARDS*, Esq; of *Highgate* aforesaid, as a Fund to answer the several Purposes hereafter mentioned; that is to say, They do hereby agree to pay or cause to be paid to all such Person or Persons who shall at any time, during the Space of One Year from the Date hereof, apprehend or take any Offender or Offenders as are herein after described, so as such Offender or Offenders may be tryed and convicted according to Law, the several and respective Rewards hereafter mentioned, in fourteen Days after Conviction, over and above what such Person or Persons may be entitled unto by such Apprehending and Conviction by Virtue of any Act or Acts of Parliament in that Case made.

For every Highwayman or Footpad who shall commit any Robbery within the said Hamlet, or any Person who shall break into any Dwelling-House in the Night-time, or send any Incendiary Letter, the Reward or Sum of Ten Pounds.

For every Person who shall steal any Horse, Mare, Colt, or other Cattle, within the said Hamlet, belonging unto the Subscribers, or commit any Theft or Robbery in the Day-time in any Dwelling-House, or break into any Out-House thereto adjoyning within the said Hamlet, and felonioufly take away to the Value of Ten Shillings, the Reward or Sum of Five Pounds.

A document dated 22 November 1737 relating to the Highgate Village Robbers Fund, to fight highwaymen, local footpads and burglars.

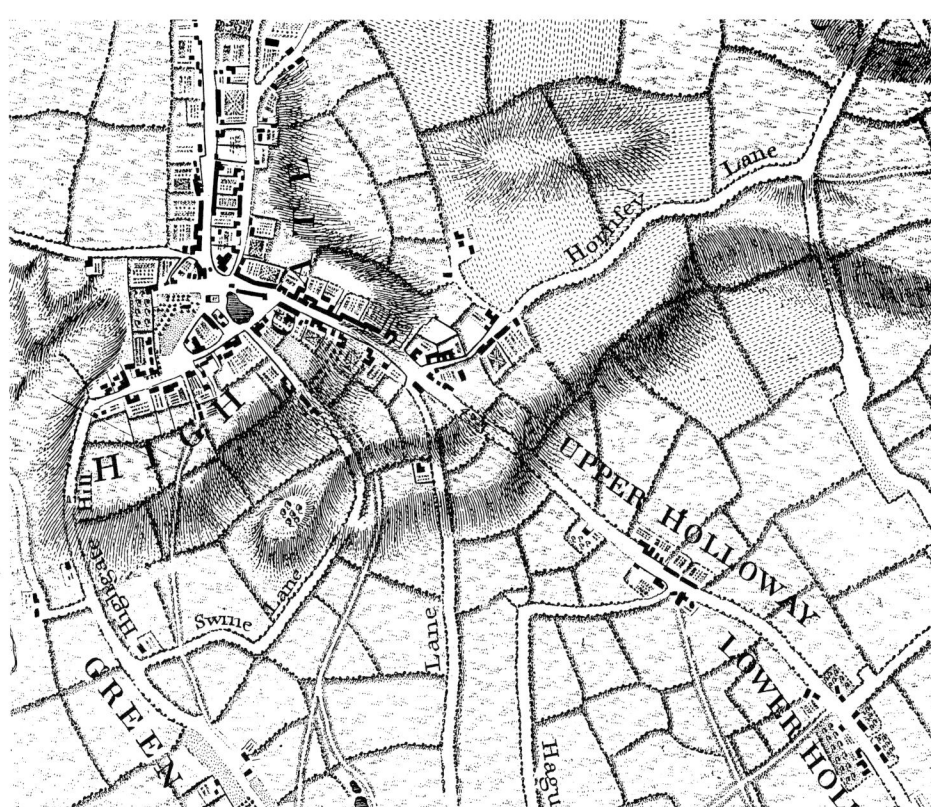

A detail from a map by John Rocque, 1745.

which (£21) was a bequest from the late Dr Atterbury. When the first pipes and buckets rotted, it was proposed that new ones be bought and be regularly tested, then hung up to dry in the chapel.

Soon afterwards (1737) they became involved in the village's so-called Robbers Fund. This fund, set by public subscription, offered rewards to those who apprehended and had convicted various categories of criminals. A highwayman, footpad, night-time burglar or sender of an 'incendiary letter' was worth £10, a horse-stealer or daytime robber £5, and a thief who stole from garden, orchard, courtyard, fish-pond etc. £2. The names of five Governors appeared below the original appeal, and one of them, John Edwards, administered the fund from its establishment until he died in 1769. Edwards was a prosperous merchant who lived at Ashurst House in South Grove and left a bequest to the almshouses. His tablet in the chapel was moved to St Michael's church in 1833; since this had been built where Ashurst House once stood, his memorial now survives on the site of one of his own living-rooms. His accounts for the Robbers Fund show many payments, the largest of £7. 1s., consisting of a £5. 10s. reward plus expenses for conducting Susannah Matthews to Hick's Hall and the Old Bayley. She was a difficult girl who had escaped the previous month on her way to court. No highwaymen were apparently caught.

Horton was succeeded as Master in 1733 by the Revd Bexworth Liptrott, of The Queen's College, Oxford, who was paid the larger salary of £30, with an extra £10 every third year 'to enable me to provide a proper person to teach

Letter to former Head Master Liptrott, 1748: 'our free school is reduced to nothing since your departure'.

writing and arithmetic', but the school was now in decline. He seemed not to have known for certain how many free scholars there should be, though he estimated that during his thirteen years there were usually between fifteen and twenty-five. Parents, he believed, were choosing instead to send children 'on their own account to the writing school' though why they should have preferred this he does not explain.

Liptrott made these admissions in February 1748, two years after he had retired, in a letter to Peter Storer, a lawyer of the Inner Temple, who had written to him: 'Our Free School is reduced to nothing since your departure and I am resolved to have it restored for the benefit of the poor and to compel the Governors by all lawful means to do their duty.' Liptrott, in reply, defended the 'integrity and honesty' of the school's Governors. He also sent Governor Edwards a copy of Storer's letter, warning him to expect an approach from Storer, and suggesting that Storer was probably 'influenced more by Chargrine, illnature and perhaps some recent disappointment, than a desire of regulating and reforming matters'.

South-east and south-west views of Highgate chapel, c. 1750.

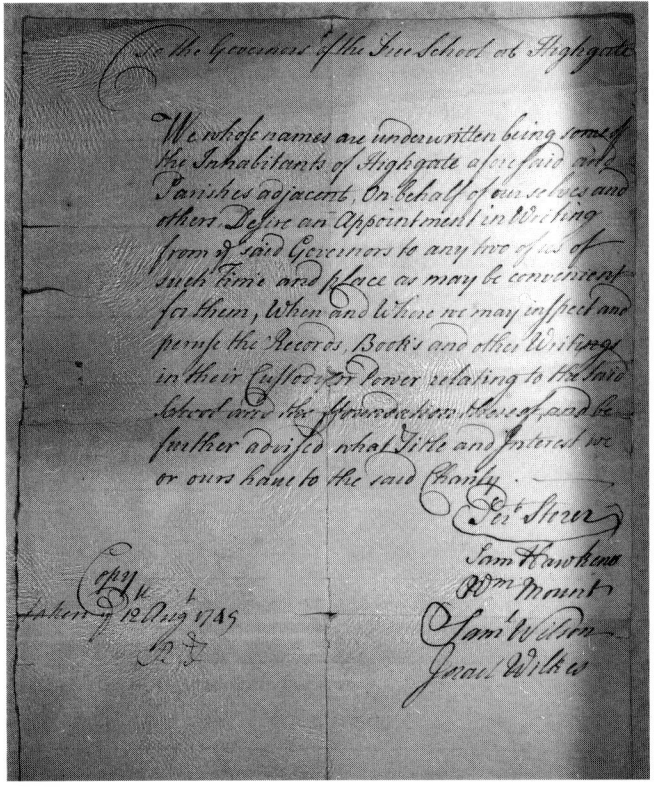

Above: *The stirring of discontent: local residents write to the Governors asking to inspect the school records, 12 August 1745.*

Above right: *A letter of recommendation from the new Head Master William Felton's fellow clergymen in Essex where Felton had been Master of the grammar school at Elmdon.*

Storer (and four others) did indeed write to the Governors, asking for an appointment and for leave to inspect 'the Records, Books and other Writings ... relating to the said School and the foundation thereof', but the Governors' answer is lost and there must have been a reconciliation since Storer himself became a Governor in 1755.

Liptrott's successor, William Felton, another graduate of The Queen's College, Oxford, was to be the longest serving Master of the eighteenth century, holding the position for thirty-four years. Felton had an academic background; his father was the Principal of St Edmund Hall, Oxford and, as an Essex rector, he had been Master of 'the Ancient Grammar School of Elmdon'. He came with an enthusiastic recommendation from four fellow clergymen of the area, and set about reviving the school. A notice displayed in Vials, a barber's shop in the High Street, read: 'This is to acquaint the Inhabitants of Highgate etc. Entitled to the Benefit of the Free-School that children may be admitted there On application to any of the Governors Where they will be taught English Writing Grammar etc in a Compleat Manner.' Felton also taught Latin, a fact confirmed by his daughter and two ex-pupils during the law case of 1823–7.

He had been in office for eight years when there arrived in Highgate the first of three members of a family which was to influence the fortunes of the school for the next sixty years: William Murray. As the 14-year-old son of a poor Scottish peer, Murray (conveniently called Mansfield, though he did not become Lord Mansfield until 1756) had come south riding a pony, his food for the two-month journey a bag of oatmeal. In London in 1718 he went to school at Westminster, and subsequently became a distinguished lawyer, prosecuting among others certain Scottish relatives who had taken part in the 1745 rebellion. In 1754 he bought Kenwood House from another Scotsman, the third Earl of Bute (George III's first and highly unpopular Prime Minister). In 1762 he became a Governor of the school.

Mansfield appears in the history of Highgate School as its enemy, but he was a civilised man, with the good taste to employ Robert Adam to reshape Kenwood, giving it the character it has today. In Bloomsbury he had a town house with a fine library. Throughout his life he was an active politician, becoming eventually leader of the House of Lords; he was a brilliant speaker, described by the *Dictionary of National Biography* as second only, 'if second', to his lifelong rival, William Pitt, Earl of Chatham. His most famous court case concerned the slave James Somersett, who was being held in irons on a ship in the Thames. The question turned on whether slavery was allowed in England, since it was not specifically forbidden, but Mansfield released Somersett on the grounds that slavery was 'so odious' that a positive law was required to permit it. Unfortunately for Mansfield he disallowed certain prosecutions of Catholics for celebrating Mass, and in 1778 was thought to have approved the Roman Catholic Relief Bill. As a result the London mob during the Gordon Riots of 1780 sacked his Bloomsbury house and burned his books. The boys of the school probably knew little of these events, four miles to the south in London, but they

A view of Highgate from Upper Holloway, 1752. The engraving seems to underestimate the severity of the incline but does give a good impression of the wide and heavily rutted droving road.

must have realised that something unusual was happening when the mob swarmed up from Hampstead, determined to destroy Kenwood. At the Spaniards, however, the landlord, Giles Thomas, opened his cellar and provided free beer which detained the rioters until the Horse Guards arrived.

In 1764, two years after Mansfield became a Governor, an incident occurred which suggested that, despite Felton's good intentions, the school was not prospering. On 25 May 1764 he wrote to Governor Edwards offering his resignation and asking for help in finding a 'chaplaincy or Church abroad'. Within three weeks he had changed his mind on the grounds that there was no prospect of getting an appointment of this sort in time to be of use to him 'in my present necessity, and, therefore I . . . Desire to continue in my duty in this place, and I will immediately make another effort for Boarders to remedy my misfortune'.

1st Earl of Mansfield – lawyer, rebuilder of Kenwood House, leader of the House of Lords and school Governor, 1762–93.

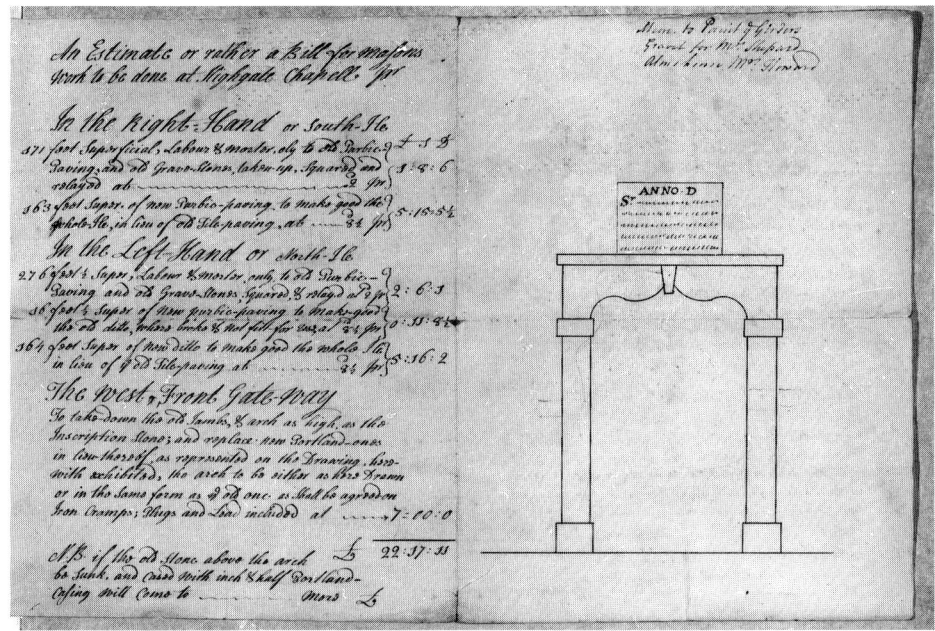

'An estimate or rather a bill for mason's work to be done at Highgate Chapell', showing a drawing of proposed west front gateway – probably from the first half of the eighteenth century.

Felton's original salary had been £20 a year plus an annual bonus which had risen by 1757 to 13 guineas, for 'his diligent and faithful discharge of his office'. The Governors then discontinued the bonus but instead, as a result of an increase of their rental income, had been able to raise his salary to £100 a year. It is therefore difficult to understand why, seven years later, he should have been in financial difficulties. That these were genuine, however, Felton's continuing anxiety about money confirms, and in 1768 Edwards told Felton, in the presence of two other Governors, that when the charity received a further increase of rental income from the reletting of a house on Ludgate Hill, his salary would again be increased. In his account of events Felton told how he waited hopefully from 10 October 1769, when the increased rents commenced, but received no rise.

Unfortunately for Felton, this was the year in which Edwards died. He had admired Edwards, and Edwards had supported him, not only in securing for him a better salary, but in maintaining that the Governors 'had no Right to Expend the Money arising from the School Estate upon the repair of the chapel'. In protest Felton wrote to four of the remaining Governors, but they referred his letter to Mansfield, and told Felton that Mansfield had studied the school charter and considered that the Master had no legal right to a rise as a result of an increase of the rental income of the charity.

Since the Governors had indeed received such an increase, Felton wrote, 'it might be inquired hereafter to what purpose this money hath been applyd'. The fact that in 1772 the chapel was entirely re-roofed and extended by incorporating into it three rooms of the schoolhouse, so making it capable of seating several hundred, provides the answer.

Nine years later, when Felton – who had stayed on despite his defeat – died

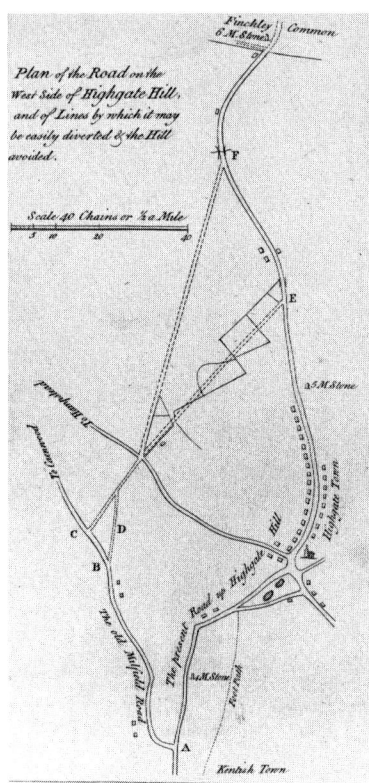

The steep gradient of Highgate Hill posed great problems to traffic, particularly as the volume increased towards the end of the eighteenth century. This map shows a proposal to build a new road circumventing the west side of the hill. It was feared that the village would suffer loss of trade if such plans went ahead.

in office, Mansfield wrote to his fellow Governor, William Bromwich (16 January 1781) a letter which makes it clear that his main concern was to find a successor who would be a satisfactory clergyman for the chapel rather than a good Master for the school. He admitted that the man he recommended, the Revd William Porter, had never taught in a school, but he had been a curate at Woolwich where he had boarded several young gentlemen and instructed them in the classics. 'I have spoken to the Arch Bishop of York,' Mansfield wrote, 'who remembers Mr Porter at Westminster School ... and that he had then a good Character ... He remembers his having acted a part in one of Terence's Plays ... with great applause; and therefore concludes that he must naturally have a good elocution.'

The school and the chapel should be separated from each other, Mansfield continued, because 'Young men of parts will dread exceedingly the engaging to revive a school which is totally gone.' Already Mansfield was suggesting a policy which, forty years later, was to provoke bitter conflict between his great nephew, the third Earl, and the school's defenders.

Few English grammar schools prospered during the eighteenth century. In 1795 Lord Kenyon wrote, 'whoever will examine the state of the grammar schools in different parts of the kingdom will see to what a lamentable condition most of them are reduced. If all persons had equally done their duty, we should not find, as is now the case, empty walls without scholars, and everything neglected but the receipt of salaries and emoluments.' More generally, it was a century during which the State still took no responsibility for education, where there was no obligation on any child to go to school, where there were few exams, and in such schools as existed no clear definition of the age of their pupils.

On the other hand it was also a period when new schools of various sorts were emerging. For the poor the Society for the Promotion of Christian Knowledge, founded in 1699, was beginning to establish charity schools. In 1780 Robert Raikes started the first of many Sunday Schools – seven years later they were estimated to be giving a quarter of a million children some kind of an education. And for lower-middle class children of Nonconformist families there were the Dissenting Academies, which, because they were less rigidly bound by their charters, often taught a broader range of subjects which could include geography, shorthand, arithmetic and science.

And though this was a period during which schools for the upper-middle classes have justly been said to have provided a 'diet of birch, boorishness, buggery and the bottle', it was also one in which some seven of them were becoming recognised as the country's 'Great Schools'. These seven included two ancient grammar schools founded within a few years of Highgate's foundation: Harrow and Rugby. At Highgate it was the diversion of its funds and its Governors' attention from school to chapel which deprived it of any chance of acquiring such a reputation.

PLATE I

A watercolour dated 1828 showing Highgate chapel with the schoolhouse beside it.

PLATE 2

The chapel in the mid-eighteenth century, an artist's impression by G. S. Shepherd painted in the 1840s, showing the Gate House tollgate on the left and Southwood Lane on the extreme right.

3

DR OWEN GOES TO LAW
1780–1833

During the eighteenth and early nineteenth century Highgate village prospered. More rich merchants and professional men from the city acquired or built houses on its airy hill-top, still surrounded by fields and woods, providing work for its relatively small proportion of labourers. It also benefited from its position on the main road to the north, where it made a convenient halt for two kinds of customer: drovers, who used it as their last stop before Smithfield Market, and coach travellers in a period when coach travel became common and the whole country networked with toll-roads.

As a result, in the early nineteenth century Highgate had no fewer than nineteen licensed public houses, at which the second sort of customer was subjected to a ritual which originated with the first: swearing on the horns. The inn would keep a pair of horns mounted on a pole in front of which the victim would be required by his 'father' to swear a long and complicated oath, eventually farcical but probably in origin part of an admission ceremony to a fraternity of drovers. Even after 1812, when Highgate Hill was bypassed by Archway Road with its gentler gradient, coaches continued to stop at Highgate's High Street inns. All in all, the village became the most prosperous part of the two parishes which it straddled.

The fortunes of Highgate School were in marked contrast. Whether or not Lord Mansfield was right in claiming in 1781 that as a grammar school it was 'entirely gone' this was a verdict which became increasingly accurate. During the next thirty-five years the Napoleonic Wars, among other things, led to a more dramatic decline in many ancient grammar schools, Highgate one of them, but at Highgate once again there was a special cause: the Master's increasing preoccupation with what was in effect becoming the parish of Highgate. In the early eighteenth century it had been the Preacher, Dr Atterbury, who was

The chapel and schoolhouse, 1814.

'A general view of Highgate from near the south-east corner of Caen Wood', by Chatelain, 1786. The chapel is just visible amongst the tree line at the centre of the print.

adopting the role of Minister of this parish. Now the Preacher became less important – Charles Mayo, the last, held the position from 1803 to 1833, but he was now merely described as Morning Lecturer – and the Governors' candidate for Minister was the Master. The Revd Thomas Bennett, a Doctor of Divinity from Trinity College, Cambridge, who succeeded Porter as Master in 1793, regularly churched women, held a monthly communion service, buried the dead in its graveyard and baptised Highgate children at their homes.

But he had a new rival: the Revd Weldon Champneys, Vicar of St Pancras. In 1805 Champneys 'called upon Dr Bennett and the Chapel Clerk for Accounts of what they have received in respect of the before mentioned duties in Pancras [i.e. the part of Highgate which lay in St Pancras parish] or in default of the same being rendered they threaten to Proceed in the Ecclesiastical Court also seem Inclined to Prohibit any of the above duties being again performed by the Chapel Reader [i.e. the Master].'

Sir John Nicholl, giving his legal opinion on Champney's claim, wrote 'I am of the opinion that Mr Champneys and the Parish Clerk cannot obtain ... any account from Dr Bennett and the Chapel Clerk of what the latter have received from the Inhabitants of Pancras.' Bennett, he considered, would be 'justified in Christening, Churching and Burying all who are brought to his Chapel for either of those purposes', but advised him to 'forbear to perform divine offices within the Parish of Pancras, except in cases of extreme necessity and for which I shd. advise him not to take any Fee'.

Despite the Master's decreasing attention to the school, it retained its forty boys (the King's School, Canterbury, by comparison, was reduced to twenty-four pupils by 1816, only eighteen of them scholars when these should have numbered fifty). But while at most grammar schools the classics were still taught, to pupils who were sons of the local gentry, farmers, tradesmen and artisans, this was not the case at Highgate. In 1816 Bennett was succeeded by the Revd Samuel Mence, a Bachelor of Divinity from Trinity College, Oxford. Mence was a well-educated and civilised man, a friend of the poet Samuel Coleridge (by this time a Highgate resident), but he never seems to have attempted or believed it his duty to make the school a grammar school.

This was shown clearly two years later, when Parliamentary Commissioners, compiling their report on the Education of the Poor, arrived at Highgate and interviewed Mence and several of the Governors.

>Quesion: What is the object of the foundation?
>Mence: To teach grammar; but I never knew it taught, and have never been applied to teach it. The words are 'libera schola grammaticalis'. I think one of the early statutes, passed six years after the foundation, provides that Latin should be taught when the scholar should arrive at a proper degree of proficiency.
>Question: What are the boys taught?
>Mence: Reading, writing and arithmetic.

The first Archway, opened in 1812, created at last an easier route round Highgate Hill; an 1830s print.

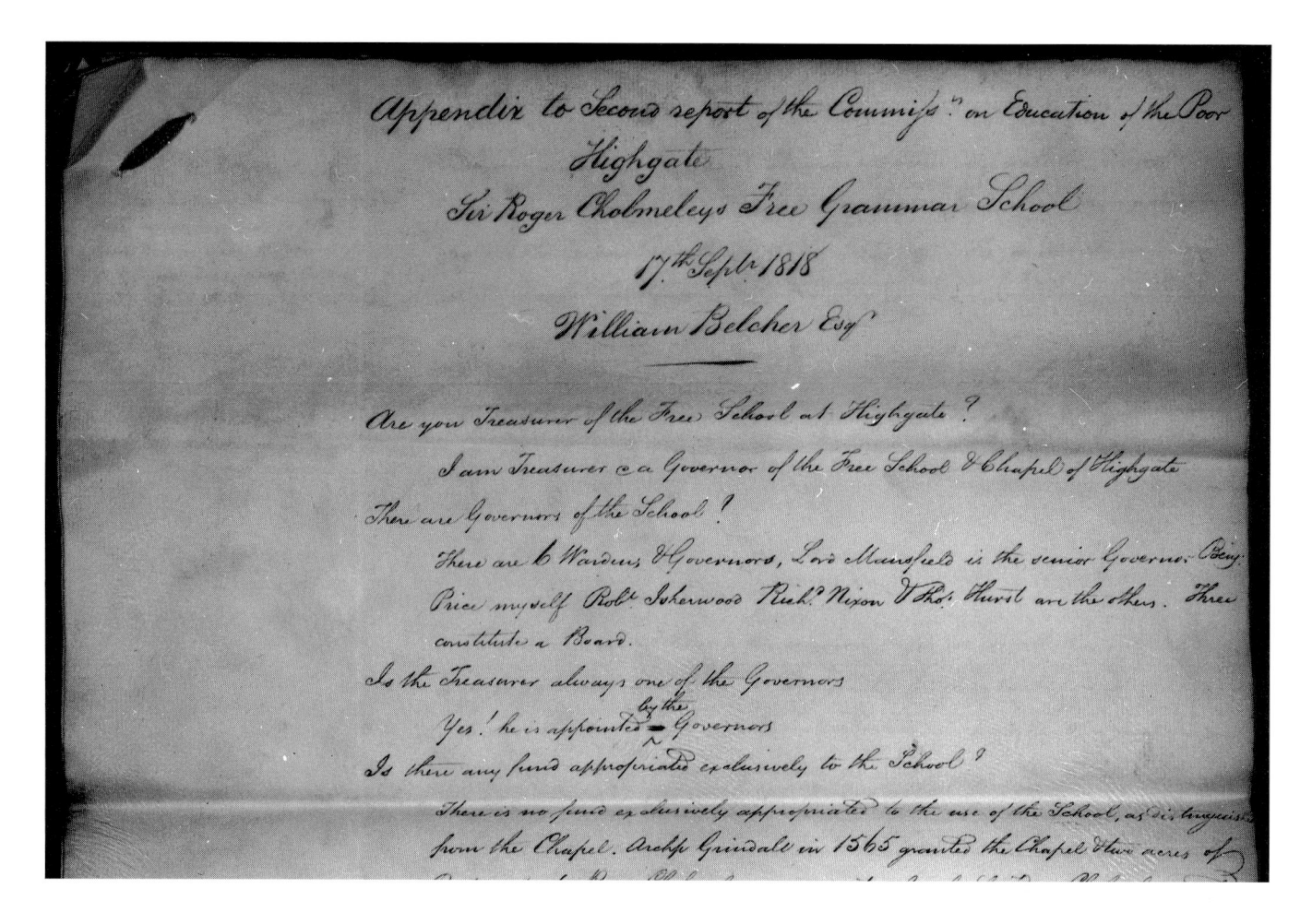

The Parliamentary Commissioners interrogate the Head Master and several of the Governors, 1818.

Question: Do you teach them yourself?
Mence: I do not.
Question: Have you any assistant?
Mence: Yes, one whom I pay. His name is Martin. I found him there, and continued him my assistant ...
Mence added that Martin was also the chapel's sexton.
Question: Do you superintend the school on any fixed days?
Mence: No, only as it is convenient to myself: I exercise authority when necessary; they are poor boys, and are frequently unmanageable. I see their parents when any quarrel arises, and interfere, in fact, whenever my assistant thinks it necessary I should do so.
Question: Of what description are the boys?
Mence: They are the sons of labouring persons; in short of such as cannot afford to pay for any other school. There is no other boys' free school at Highgate. If my school were sufficiently large, I think it probable that many boys would come to me instead of going to the dissenters' school. I found this opinion upon observing that boys willingly come from their schools to mine when there is a vacancy.

In answer to other questions Mence said that there were forty pupils at the school, admitted between the ages of 7 and 14, by application to the Governors. There was usually a waiting list. Besides the forty free scholars he kept four borders.

> Question: Have your private pupils any communication with this school?
> Mence: None whatever; they are generally young men who have left public schools, and are preparing by me for the university.

His assistant, Martin, however, kept ten 'pay-boys' who were 'taught in the school with the other forty'.

The school formed part of Mence's own house. It was 'not large, it cannot well accommodate forty boys. The desks are crowded, the ceiling low; there is not air enough, it is unwholsomely close in the summer.'

Mence paid his assistant £20 a year but planned to increase this now that his own salary had been increased from £100 to £200 (twenty years later the incomes of 5,000 English clergy were still under £200 a year). Asked to justify his own

The chapel and schoolhouse in the early nineteenth century.

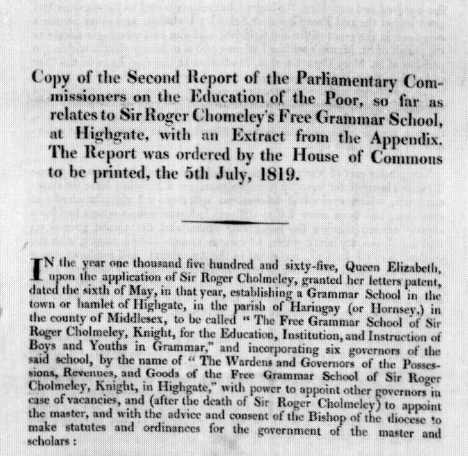

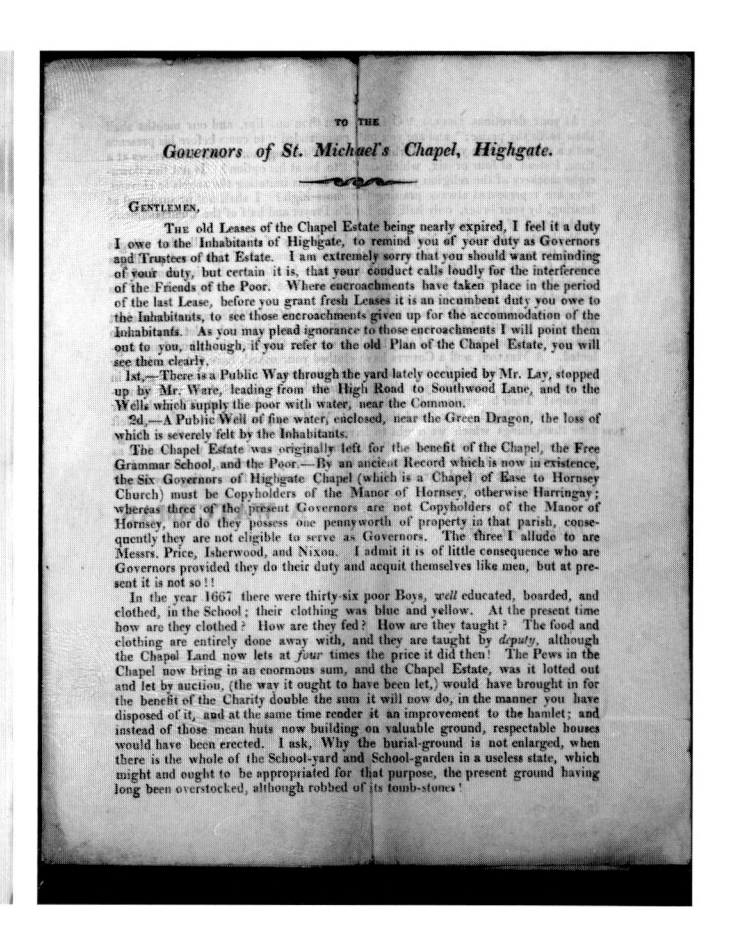

Above: *The report of the Parliamentary Commissioners, 1819.*

Above right: *An anonymous circular accusing the Governors of mismanagement, 1817.*

increase, Mence explained that he was also reader and afternoon preacher in the chapel. Asked a similar question, one of the Governors, Robert Isherwood, replied, 'The augmentation was not only in his character as schoolmaster, but as morning reader and afternoon preacher; he has much parochial duty.' Clearly Mence, like Bennett, was acting as Highgate's parson, an arrangement which Isherwood did not question. Freeing Mence from teaching was essential if he was to have such a role.

When the Commissioners questioned the Treasurer, William Belcher, about the charity's funds, they found confusion. Belcher admitted that there was 'no fund exclusively to the use of the school, as distinguished from the chapel' and the accounts also included receipts and payments on behalf of the girls' charity school and the almshouses. The Governors agreed to separate these, and were able to clear up some of the confusion. The result showed that there was no shortage of money, and this enabled them to respond quickly to the Commissioners' criticisms of the school's premises. On 19 March 1819, Belcher told them,

> The governors having the concurrence of the Bishop of London, are about to erect a new school-room on an enlarged scale, capable of holding a hundred boys, to be instructed on the plan used in the National schools. This appropriation of a part of their surplus revenue, they flatter

themselves, the commissioners will agree with them in thinking, is perfectly consistent with the design of the founder.

The Commissioners had been told of this proposal before they published their report and though they admitted that, as a grammar school, Highgate had 'fallen into complete decay', they on the whole approved, concluding that in the circumstances it would be best to continue 'the inferior mode of education now pursued and proposed'. Not so a certain Dr Henry Butts Owen, who had been a candidate for Master in 1816 when Mence was chosen. The Sunday after Mence's appointment, Owen had told him that he had 'entered a caveat against him ... with the Bishop of London'; the Bishop, as a result, had made enquiries about the connection between the school and the chapel, and the rights of the Governors.

Soon afterwards (1817) an anonymous pamphleteer of Highgate, who signed himself 'A Watchman', published a circular addressed to Governor Isherwood. 'I am extremely sorry that you should want reminding of your duty, but certain it is, that your conduct calls loudly for the interference of the Friends of the Poor.'

The Governors, Watchman continued, had closed a right of way 'leading from the High Road to Southwood Lane' then to the wells which supplied the poor with water near the Common, and had 'enclosed a Public Well of fine water ... near the Green Dragon'. They had also neglected the school. 'In the year 1667 there were thirty-six Boys *well* educated, boarded and clothed, in the School; their clothing was blue and yellow. At the present time how are they clothed? How are they fed? How are they taught? The food and clothing are entirely done away with, and they are taught by *deputy* ...'

'Let me beg of you', Watchman concluded, 'to *alter* your conduct as Governors, and act more consistent with the religion you profess, or be assured an injunction will be applied for and obtained.'

View towards Islington and the City from Highgate Hill, early nineteenth century.

When the Governors set about investigating their legal rights and obligations, it soon emerged that they were doing so for another reason: to justify spending their funds on repairing and if possible enormously enlarging the chapel, the present one being, they claimed, again in a ruinous condition. The Bishop of London encouraged them, writing on 14 May 1818, 'it seems reasonable that the Chapel, as part of the fabric, should be repaired from the funds of the Establishment'. He made another suggestion. If the chapel were to be sufficiently enlarged to make it into a church, 'the new Act for building Churches', or 'the Society for building Churches' might contribute to the cost. He would encourage 'any arrangement that without injuring the School is calculated to benefit the Parishioners'.

On 8 July, however, he wrote to Governor Isherwood, 'I wish the Governors would take an opinion generally on the whole in order to learn whether a reference to Chancery will be sufficient – and whether an Act of Parliament may not be necessary and which I think it will – if it shall appear that ... the property conveyed by Bp Grindall is – as I suspect – unsound.'

The Parliamentary Commissioners had come and gone, the new schoolroom with space for over a hundred poor boys had been opened and sexton Martin had been sent to the Central School to learn how to teach them by the so-called Madras System (in which older boys taught younger) by the time the Governors decided that an Act of Parliament would indeed be needed, and on 10 August 1821 they announced that they intended to apply for one. It would not only have allowed them to pull down the old chapel and replace it with a much larger one, extending from North Road to Southwood Lane and occupying almost the whole of the present North Road quadrangle, and to use the school's surplus assets for this work, but also to raise a village rate.

A fortnight later (27 August) there happened to be a public meeting for another pupose at Highgate, and it was here that 'the storm which had long been gathering burst at once' (John Green). Owen and his supporters formed a committee which held its first meeting on 13 September, and a day or two later wrote to the Governors asking for information about the proposed Bill and about 'the nature and amount' of the charities which they managed.

On 17 September the Governors replied that they would show 'ignorance of their office if they were to allow themselves to be called to account by individuals, though ever so respectable, having no jurisdiction over their conduct'. On 18 October the committee wrote again, but got a similar answer. And in December they made a private approach but again without success.

Meanwhile, in October the Bishop of London had remained cautious, asking for time to consult a legal acquaintance. But by December he had made up his mind and sent the Governors a long letter of support. If they were influenced by this he must take some of the responsibility for their obstinacy and its consequences, since it contained various tendentious opinions and inaccuracies. For example, he used the school's statutes of 1571 as evidence that the chapel had been a chapel of ease *before* the founding of the school, and asserted that the statutes were drawn up 'according to the directions of the Founder', an unsafe assumption since, by 1571, Cholmeley had been dead for six years. Nevertheless

Above left: *The Governors respond to criticism, 1821: 'they have nothing to conceal'.*

Above: *'An Epistle ...', the most famous document relating to the 'trouble'. It was a defence of the Governors in response to the pamphleteer John Green.*

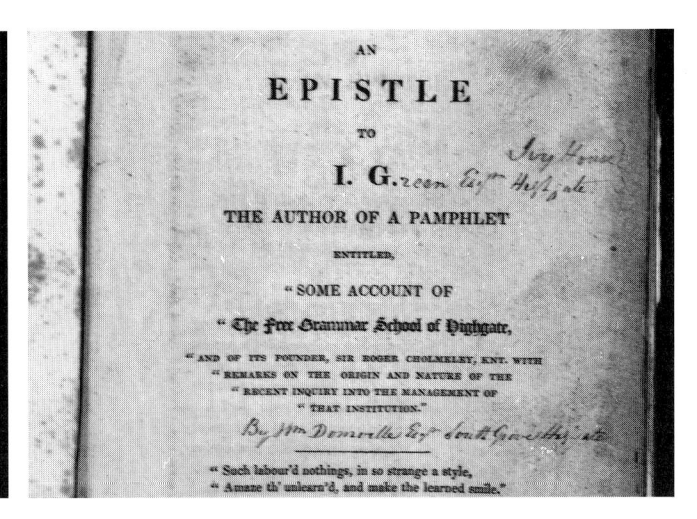

the Governors circulated the Bishop's letter around Highgate, and entered a caveat with the Attorney General in an attempt to forestall an approach to him by the committee.

When they brought their Bill before Parliament it was first passed by the Lords, then, despite violent attacks from Brougham, passed its first two readings in the Commons. In Committee, however, where members of the Highgate committee were allowed to put their case, it was proposed that a new chapel be built on a new site, the Minister to be appointed by the Bishop of London, and the school to receive pew rents. Rather than accept such proposals the Governors withdrew the Bill.

In order to prevent it being re-presented, the committee now persuaded the Attorney General (something of a formality) to join them in an action against the Governors in the Court of Chancery.

About the same time pamphlets began to appear in Highgate some supporting the Governors, some against them. Against were those of John Green of Ivy House, writing under the initials I.G., who published *A Brief Account of the Free Grammar School,* and *Some Account of the Grammar School of Highgate* (1822), the second a revised version of the first, expanded to eighty-five pages. He drew particular attention to a phrase in Cholmeley's grant of his London properties to the charity, which he gave it 'for the better maintenance of the said Grammar School, and not otherwise, or to any other uses'. He insisted that the committee had done its best to come to an agreement with the Governors, but their attempts had been 'all unfortunately unsuccessful: the answers of the governors, evincing ... a loftiness of tone, but little likely either to advance their claims to public confidence and support or "to buy golden opinions of the people".

'To this demeanour may be attributed, in a great measure, the subsequent disunion in the hamlet; had the governors not refused all investigation and arrangement; had they but accepted the hand of conciliation held out to them to the very last ... how much of public advantage might have been obtained, how much of private discord prevented!'

Copies of Green's two pamphlets, bound together with other documents concerning the case, are preserved in the school's archives. All have been heavily and sardonically annotated by someone who supported Dr Owen and was hostile to the Governors. Against the opening words of the Governors' letter to Owen of 17 September 1821, which read 'The Governors of Highgate School ...', he wrote 'And pray why not *Grammar*? The Governors seem to have a vast horror of this word! they have quite erased it from their Vocabulary.' Where the Governors wrote that they 'have no wish to press a rate on the Hamlet without its concurrence', he wrote, 'See. How kind and considerate.'

Next year a pamphlet entitled *An Epistle to I.G.*, by A.Z., argued vigorously in support of the Governors. A handwritten note on the title page of one of the school's copies read 'said to have been written by Mr Domville, partner with Mr Kinderley who is not only a Governor but also solicitor to their proceedings!!!'

A.Z. had 'all along felt convinced of the integrity' of the Governor's motives, and had 'witnessed, therefore, with indignation, not the war which has been waged, but the mode, the uncivilized, the dishonourable mode of warfare which has been employed against them.' The chapel, he wrote, had always been a chapel of ease and the intentions of Cholmeley and Grindal had been as much to co-operate in supporting the chapel as to found a school. About the school itself, he wrote:

> Considering then how decidedly elementary is the sort of instruction prescribed by the statutes; considering also the very slender evidence which exists of Sir Roger Cholmeley's school having been at any time, in the common acceptation of the word, a grammar school; and the long usage which can be proved of a different and inferior system of education having been pursued, it may well be questioned whether [it would be possible] to establish in its place a school for teaching the classics.

The Attorney General's two cases – in practice those of Owen and his committee members – against Mansfield, his fellow Governors and the Revd Samuel Mence, first came to the Court of Chancery between 16 December 1823 and 17 January 1824. In presenting their arguments they rehearsed the complaints of the committee: that Governors ought to have considered the Free Grammar School the 'main object' of the charity which Cholmeley had founded, but instead had considered the 'Chapel and the performance of services therein for the general use of the Inhabits of Highgate as the main and principal objects of the sd Charity'; that there was no reason to think the chapel had been a chapel of ease before the statutes of 1571 declared it to be one, and no reason to think that Grindal had any other purpose in giving it to Cholmeley than to provide it for the use of the school; that the Governors had

> for many years applied and expended a very small portion of the revenues of sd Charity for the maintainance and benefit of said School but have expended the greater part of the Revenues reced by them ... in repairg and making more comodious said Chapel'; [that the Governors had] 'never kept or produced to the psons interested in said Charits any correct account of the receipts or expenditure theof and on the contrary have so intermixed

such receipts and expenditure with the Receipts and Expenditures of other Charities of which they are Trustees so as to make it extremely difficult if not impossible to ascertain ... how or in what manner or for what purposes ... the funds and revenues of the said Grammar School have in fact been laid out.

Meanwhile the Master had turned over the teaching in the school to his sexton, given the great majority of his time to what had in effect become his parish of Highgate, and entirely failed to maintain the school as the grammar school which Cholmeley had intended to found.

They added that the Governors had grossly mismanaged the funds and assets of the trust; in particular in 1818, when 'a considerable quantity of land very advantageously situated for building upon ... came into their hands' they had 'let the said Lands for the erection and Buildg of small houses or cottages fit only to be inhabited by the Poorer Class of people and that in consequence ... a vast number of poor and indigent people have been introduced in the sd hamlet to the great deterioration of the respectability of the neighbourhood.' As for Mence, he had treated the chapel 'as a mere parochial chapel unconnected and independent of sd free Grammar School', while the sexton, with the knowledge and permission of Mence and the Governors, had received 'for his own benefit from the Scholars ... sums of money ... under the pretence of the same being an Admissn to said School'.

Mence admitted to the court that when he was appointed he had been 'wholly ignorant' of the statutes of the school. He knew from Felton's daughter that Felton had taught a class of four to six boys Latin, but considered that in general the school had been 'totally perverted' from the original intentions of the founder. 'None of the Inhabts of Highgate or its vicinity', he claimed, had 'ever expressed a wish to have their Children instructed in Grammar or Classical learning at sd School.' 'In consequence of his sitn as reader at sd Chapel', he had 'become looked up to by sevl persons who are in the habit of attending the same ... as the person from whom they have a right to expect the performance of divers ... Clerical duties.'

In defending themselves the Governors claimed that they 'verily believed that sd School and Chapel formed ... one foundatn the School being for the educatn and instructn of the Childn of the Town or Hamlet of Highgate and its vicinity and the Chapel for the Ease and accommodatn of the Inhabts' and that when the Governors of the time accepted Sir Roger Cholmeley's gift of the chapel they 'imposed upon themselves ... an Obligatn to see that the duties of sd Chapel were properly pformed'.

They denied many of the committee's accusations, claiming, for example, that they had been told by pupils that no Latin was taught in Felton's time, and explained that they had merely continued to run the sort of school which they had discovered when they became Governors.

The following Easter term (1824) Lord Chancellor Eldon gave his opinion on the legal situation, and expressed his hope that this would settle the matter. It did not, as the *Morning Chronicle*'s report of 3 February 1825 makes clear. 'The friends of the Charity [Dr Owen and his committee], relying too much upon

Lord Eldon's decree: the Lord Chancellor's decision on the Governors' management – he came out in support of Dr Owen and the existing Governors.

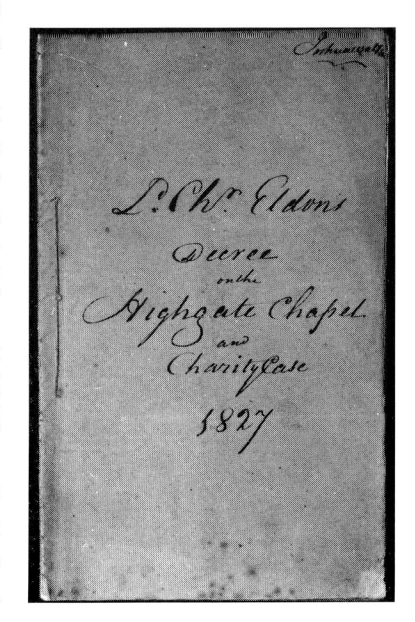

View towards the school, 1827.

the weight which the Lord Chancellor's opinion ought to have with the Trustees, did not press for a decree; and what was the consequence ...? The School still remains in its ruinous and degraded state; the gravedigger is still in office, and the charter is a dead letter!' As a result, exactly three years after the original actions the Attorney General and committee had to go to court again and Lord Eldon only finally issued his decree on 13 April 1827.

His decision was clear: 'The charity ... founded by Sir Roger Cholmeley is a charity for the sustenance and maintainance of a Free Grammar School for teaching the learned Languages' and its Governors 'are not bound further to enlarge the Chapel'.

He referred to the Master of the court the working out of the consequences of his decision. The Master should report fully on the charity's assets and on how they should be applied, should approve a scheme 'for the future management and regulating of the charity', and should decide whether 'any good and valid appointment of a master' of the school existed and if so whether he had 'fulfilled the Duties of his office agreably to the Statutes'.

4

DR DYNE – SECOND FOUNDER
1838–1874

APART FROM QUEEN ELIZABETH'S original founding grant, Lord Eldon's judgment was the greatest single event in the history of Highgate School. It led to Highgate's re-establishment as a grammar school, and in 1832 to new statutes. Like the original ones, these offered places to forty free scholars, but now required unambiguously that they should be given a grammar school education. To ensure that they were fit for this they would have to prove themselves proficient in the three Rs. Once admitted they would be primarily taught the classics, but for £8 a year they could learn other subjects, taught by masters specially engaged for the purpose. In addition to the free scholars, the Head Master could take 'pay-boys' at twelve guineas a year. At first these were to number no more than fifty but in July 1832 this limit was abolished. They were not to be 'formed into distinct classes but treated in all respects' like the free scholars.

As for the chapel, it was not merely to cease to be a chapel of ease for the village; by an Act of Parliament dated 17 June 1830 the Governors were to be allowed to demolish it, and to contribute £2,000 to a new village church (also confusingly to be called St Michael's). There pews were to be reserved for the students, Governors and Masters, and for the next thirty-five years the school had no chapel of its own. Mence continued to be the school's Master, but also became the incumbent of the new St Michael's. Though he managed at first to recruit thirty-two pupils, by the time he resigned in 1838 they had dwindled to nineteen.

So it happened, in the year when Victoria was crowned (and 1,200 Highgate villagers sat down to a celebration feast at tables 900 ft. long in North Road) that the Governors chose for the new Head Master the man who was to take proper advantage of the school's new statutes. Many nineteenth-century schools

The 'troubles' resolved: an Act to demolish the chapel and allow the Governors to contribute to a church for the village.

The interior of the new Highgate church in 1833. Until the building of the present school chapel in 1866 the school had no private chapel.

Dr John Bradley Dyne, Head Master 1838–74.

had one great and transforming headmaster: Butler of Shrewsbury, Arnold of Rugby, Thring of Uppingham, Percival of Clifton, Cotton of Marlborough, Mitchinson of the King's School, Canterbury, to name a few. The Revd John Bradley Dyne was such a man, and what he achieved in his thirty-six years at Highgate was one of the greatest transformations.

At the time of his appointment Dyne was a 29 year old Fellow of Wadham College, Oxford. He had been brought up in Somerset where he went to King Edward's School, Bruton. After four years at Oxford he won only a second-class degree, but nevertheless became a Fellow two years later. In 1835 and 1836 he took holy orders and in 1837 was made Dean of the College. The Warden of Wadham at this time, Symonds, was an opponent of the religious views of Newman and Keble which were currently disturbing Oxford, but there is no evidence that Dyne was out of sympathy with him. On the contrary, in a Catholic missal Dyne wrote that he had bought it to study the beliefs of the Church of Rome so that 'I might (by the Grace of God) be enabled to refute them'. He more probably left Oxford because he wanted to marry, something he could not do as a college Fellow.

At Highgate he had not been the Governors' automatic choice. When they met on 6 August 1838 they considered thirteen candidates and first voted, three for and three against Dyne, then three for and three against the Revd James Gillman. Governor Cooper, as Chairman, now claimed a casting vote in Gillman's favour, but other Governors challenged his right to this – had they not done so the school must have had a very different future. Six weeks later (24 September) they unanimously elected Dyne.

Dyne's achievement at Highgate is most clearly shown by the rise in its numbers. By 1850 the nineteen Mence had left had grown to 104. Twelve years later there were 126 and the Governors minuted, 'If Dr Dyne with little or no parentage, could raise the school to its present numbers it may not unreasonably be presumed that the present or future Headmasters may with its present considerable parentage effect a still further addition to the numbers in the school.' They were right. During his last twelve years the school grew to 160. In one of those years, 1867, when the new buildings were ready, fifty-eight new boys arrived.

In part Dyne was lucky. The 1840s and 1850s were years when an increasing number of British middle-class parents decided to send their sons to public schools, not to their local schools. Many well known public schools were then founded, starting with Cheltenham in 1840, soon followed by Marlborough, Wellington, Haileybury, Clifton and half a dozen others. Highgate, it could be argued, was the sort of local school which should have suffered as a result, but Dyne in fact soon began to attract boys from elsewhere. The railways, which first made it easy in these years to send boys to distant schools, and which are sometimes offered as the explanation of the growth of public schools, enabled Highgate to extend the area it served.

The more probable reason for public school expansion – that merchants, manufacturers and members of the professions who had climbed to prosperity during the Industrial Revolution wished to ensure that their sons should grow up gentlemen – might seem just as unlikely to have benefited Highgate. Dyne's achievement was to persuade such parents that his school could do this for their boys.

Most importantly, he had to convince them that the school's academic standards were adequate, and to ensure this he soon established a regular examination of the school by an outside examiner. On 18 June 1842 the Governors minuted, 'The annual examination of the Boys in the Grammar School took place this day by Dr Russell, Geo. Kinderley Esq., Rev T. H. Causton and W. D. C. Cooper Governors present.' For many years the Revd John Russell was the regular examiner.

But Dyne also realised that the best proof of the school's standards was the securing of places at Oxford and Cambridge. He was soon succeeding. From the first 225 boys to arrive in his time, forty-three sooner or later obtained Oxford

Admissions register showing the admission of Gerard Manley Hopkins and the generally high social standing of pupils' families.

School library register, 1862; judging by the withdrawals, Gerard Manley Hopkins was a keen student.

or Cambridge degrees. To enable talented Highgate boys to go to Oxford and Cambridge he persuaded the Governors to establish a £50 exhibition. In 1846 the first exhibitioner, R. E. Waters, went appropriately to Dyne's old College, Wadham. Waters became an antiquarian and genealogist.

The 'gentlemen residents' of Highgate now came to the aid of the school, voting at a meeting in the schoolroom on 3 March 1846 that three more university exhibitions of £50 each be established, to be paid for partly by public donation, partly by an annual charge on parents. To this the Governors agreed, though making the parents' contributions voluntary. In April 1851 the examiner of the school reported, 'I have but to repeat this year the testimony which I gave last year to the proficiency of the whole school, and to the superiority of Charles Griffith among the Boys of the senior form, and his fitness to be sent to the university with an Exhibition.'

In the following years many open scholarships to Oxford and Cambridge were also won: between 1855 and 1865 no fewer than twenty out of 286 entrants to the school, and in Dyne's time as a whole forty-nine out of 1,100 entrants. Scholarship winners included the poet, Gerard Manley Hopkins, and the translator, Philip Worsley. Worsley's 'splendid translations of Homer's *Odyssey* into Spenserian stanzas' was directly inspired, the Revd Walter Skeat believed, by Dyne's teaching. 'Our head-master had one somewhat uncommon idea, which savoured ... of great wisdom. Instead of invariably requiring us to turn English poetry into Latin verse, he sometimes gave us pieces of Latin poetry to turn into English verse; a change which was delightful and refreshing. The

PLATE 3

A tinted engraving of Highgate, 1814.

PLATE 4

Right: *Hand-drawn map of the parish of Hornsey, c. 1827. The school was fortunate that the suburbs had not encroached by the time playing fields were needed. Senior Field was leased in 1848.*

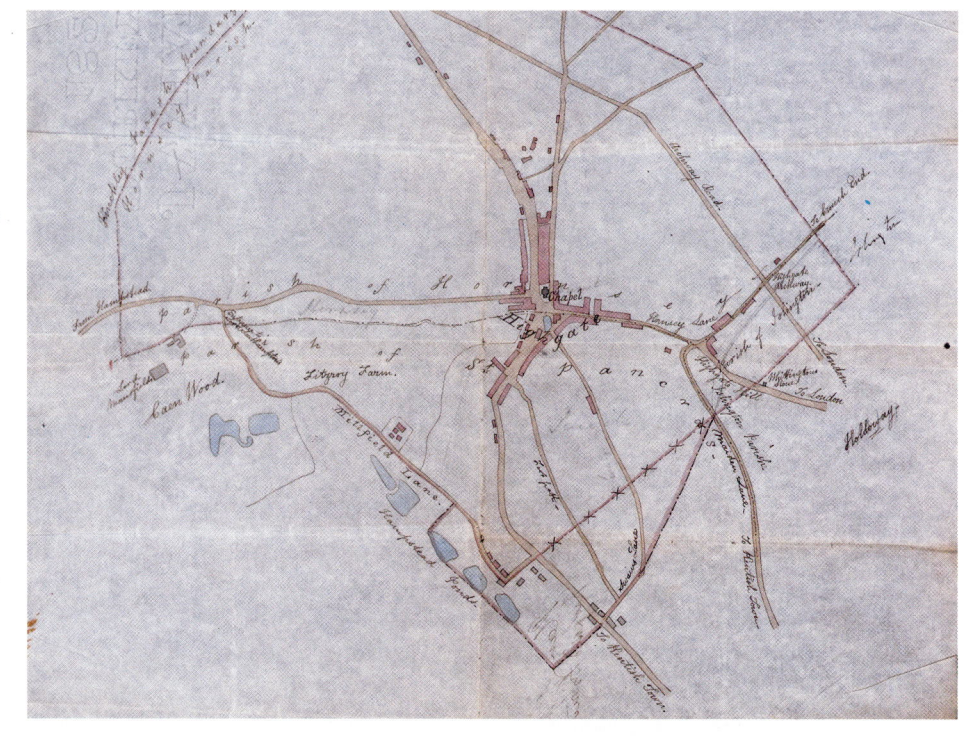

Below: *'View from the slopes of Highgate Archway', 1822, by Thomas Baynes. The explosive development of Islington and Camden, which would unite Highgate with the capital, was about to begin.*

English verse was usually poor enough, but the attempt to produce it was stimulating and valuable.' In other ways, however, Dyne's teaching methods were old fashioned. The school's Greek and Latin grammars were 'written in Latin'. His way of marking was by letters: 'O,' Optime, representing 3 good marks; B, Bene, 2; Satis, 1; Nil, 0; Vix, 1 bad mark; Male, 2; Pessime, 3.' Dyne, according to Edmund Yates (1840–6), later an actor and journalist, 'thought the study of Latin and Greek the principal objects of our creation' (it was Yates who, as editor of the *Comic Times*, asked Charles Dodgson to use a pen-name, and out of the four which Dodgson suggested, chose Lewis Carroll). He never liked Yates because he was not a 'show-boy', who would go to university and reflect credit on the school's teaching.

In the 1840s a so-called 'writing and English master' was employed, but as late as 1858 Francis Tatham remembered that there was still 'no teaching of English literature or science'. As for modern languages, Yates remembered that

> the learning of French and German was an 'extra' ... supposed to be paid for separately, and to be undergone by the boys whose foolish parents insisted on their acquiring it, at times when the rest of the school was at play. A snuff-taking old French gentleman came once a week, and sat at the end of a table, while a dozen boys fought round it, larked, and shot paper pellets into his frizzy hair. He had no authority, poor old fellow, and there was no one to keep order.

It was only in 1857 that Dr Muncke arrived to teach French and German. He was a retired Prussian officer who had been lanced in the shoulder by a Frenchman at Waterloo, a wound which 'he often described, and which, as a great privilege, we were allowed to feel'. But if Highgate was not ahead in broadening its curriculum, it was not particularly behind. Marlborough and Rossall, among the first to establish 'modern sides', only did so in 1854.

As the number of boys in the school increased the schoolroom which the Governors had built in 1819–20 became less and less adequate. In March 1844 Dyne drew the Governors' attention to this problem and also to the state of his own house. A year later the Governors agreed to have the schoolroom extended, the Head Master's house pulled down, its site made into a playground, and a new house bought for him from the estate of Mr Bloxham, a Governor who had recently died. This stood at the far side of Southwood Lane, on the site now occupied by Dyne House. As part of these arrangements, Dyne lent the Governors £1,000, interest free, for his lifetime, on condition they spent £400 on improving his new house.

Until now the four forms into which the school was divided had all been taught, as at many schools of the time, in a single large hall, known at Highgate as Big School, their different masters competing to be heard. Now Big School was extended by adding a classroom to its southern end on the same level, with a library above. Entering from its northern door, a boy of the time remembered that Forms Four and Five were on the left, with their master seated between them, Forms One and Two on the right with their master in front of them. The room was lighted by two large windows looking east and west.

A print from the 1850s showing the pre-1865 schoolhouse.

There was also another window, a much smaller affair, high up opposite the door. It belonged to the library ... and gave no light to the big schoolroom, but through it the Head Master could see what was going on in the large room below ... This window gave a peculiar jingle and rattle when opened, the effect of which made everyone in the room below suddenly very attentive and studious. Sometimes a youngster sent upstairs to report himself for bad conduct, would have the good luck not to find the doctor in the library. Then, the spirit of mischief entering into him, he would rattle the window and immediately dart behind the wall to escape detection, enjoying the fact that he, a small cause, had produced a great effect in a large room.

At this time two or three other classrooms were loosely attached to the southern end of Big School, but it was the library with the doctor's internal window that boys remembered best.

At its opposite end another window looked down on the large playground. This was separated from Southwood Lane by a wall which, because of the slope of the ground, was 4 ft. high on the school side and 12 ft. high on the lane side. The playground included the ruins of the old chapel, one part of which was used as a fives court, while the other was 'overgrown with very thick ivy, than which I do not remember to have ever seen finer. By its means we were enabled to climb to a great height all over the wall after the fives balls which got lodged in its branches.' To the playground an ancient character called Sodger came daily to sell 'oranges and a peculiar kind of sweet-meats called cushions. Poor old Sodger died before the demolition of the old premises. He was buried by a subscription among the boys!' The school probably owes it pre-eminence at fives to the chapel ruins. Interestingly the Eton form of the game which it adopted had also developed against Eton's chapel walls. In the 1830s fives seems to have been Highgate's most formal game, though hockey of a sort was played in the playground. Less formal games included 'chevy' (a sort of Prisoners' Base), 'hoppy', 'cross touch' and rounders, while the lobby which stood just inside the North Road gate was 'much used by the smaller boys as a playing-room, especially adapted to the spinning of peg-tops'.

In October 1848, however, the Governors considered for the first time acquiring a playground for more organised games, and accepted an offer from Governor George Crawley of the lease of a field in Hampstead Lane at £30 a year for twenty-one years. The agreement was backdated to 1847, and was said to be for 'the field now used as a Playground'. It seems likely, therefore, that 1847 was the year in which organised games were first played at Highgate. Certainly by 1849 the school had a cricket eleven, and this field eventually became the Senior Field.

It was by no means ahead in the introduction of formal games. Eton first played Westminster at cricket in 1796 and Winchester played Harrow in 1825. School football remained a far more haphazard affair, as the famous description of the School House game in *Tom Brown's Schooldays* at Rugby during Arnold's time (the 1830s) shows. Nor do inter-school cricket matches (which were

The earliest known Speech Day programme, 1851.

One of the earliest existing photos of the school Rugby football XV, 1864.

probably played by school clubs) mean that games permeated school life as they came to permeate it during the second half of the century. At Marlborough in the 1840s it was estimated that only a fifth of the boys played games, while the rest spent their free time wandering the countryside, trespassing and poaching. It was to curtail activities of this sort that headmasters in the 1850s began to impose organised and eventually compulsory games on their schools.

Such a development required more (and more securely held) playgrounds. At Highgate in August 1857 the Treasurer told the other Governors that he had bought a five-acre lot from the Highgate estate of a Miss Jones, 'thinking it would be desirable to secure that land for the purpose of a permanent Cricket Ground'. There was also the possibility of acquiring a further ten acres from the same estate. The Governors accepted Dyne's suggestion that the school should buy the first lot, and that the second lot be bought by subscription. To this Dyne contributed the greatest share, and in 1859 both lots were put into the names of Dyne and Governor Charles Bloxham, the other main subscriber, to be held in trust for the school. The final stage in these transactions was an offer by Crawley to swap the school's new five-acre lot for the playing-field it was renting from him. The school was thus able to retain its original cricket ground.

The properties which the school now had in Hampstead Lane led to a proposal

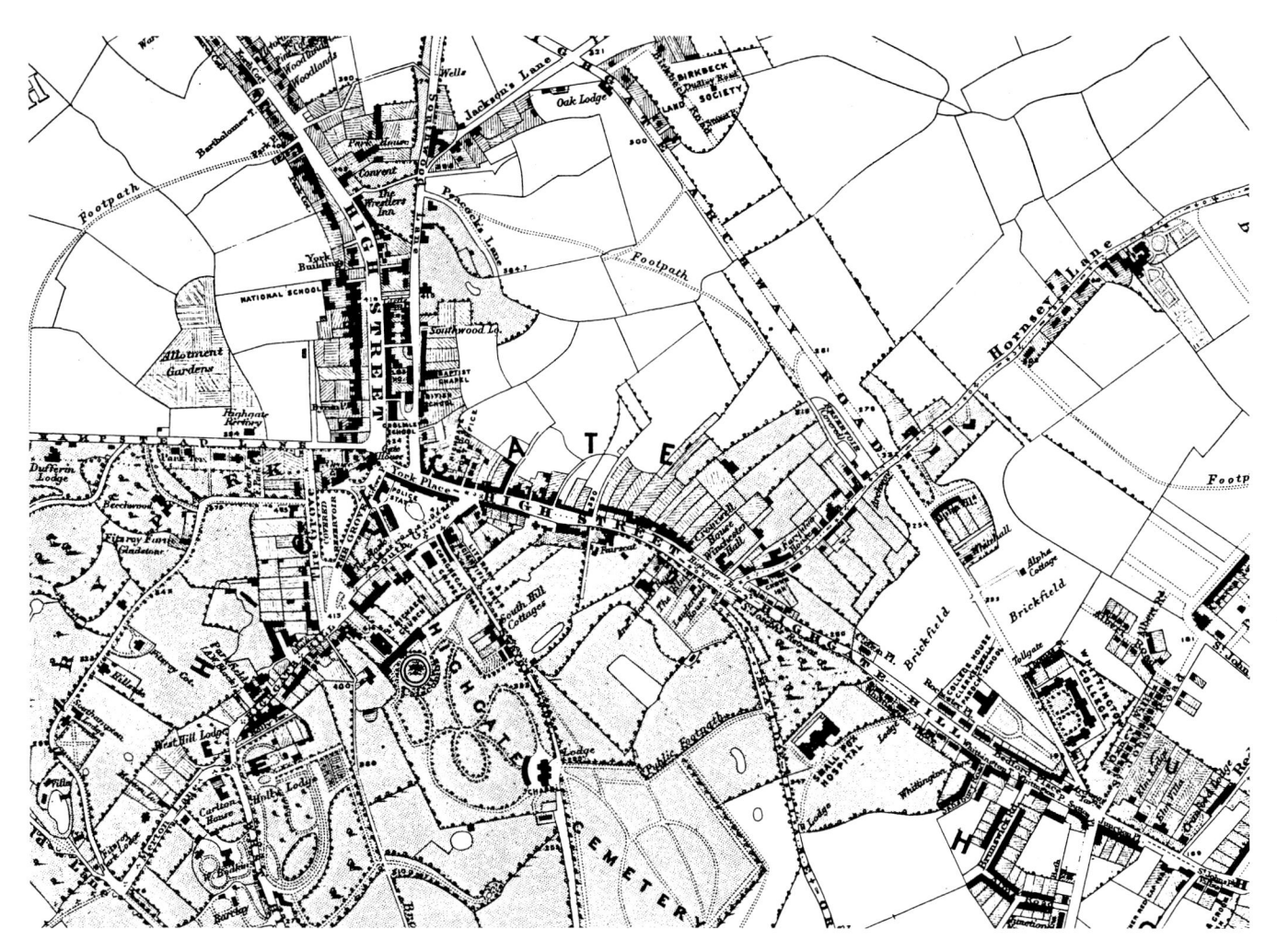

Stanford's 1862 map of London's northern suburbs shows open fields still running right up to the High Street. Estates of housing quickly followed the opening of the railway to Archway and Finchley in 1867.

which, if it had been agreed, would have entirely transformed the school. On 16 April 1862 William Ford, a recently elected Governor, submitted to his fellow Governors a memorandum proposing that the school should abandon its ancient site and move to this new area.

Now that the school was so much larger, Ford argued, it badly needed more buildings. The most obvious way to provide these was to build on the home playground, but this was already barely large enough, and if the chapel were ever rebuilt on its old site would be further reduced. Demolishing neighbouring houses which the school owned and building on their sites would seriously diminish its income. Moving away, on the other hand, would have the opposite effect, since it would release for building land at the village's centre which was of great value. There would be other advantages. Since the early 1850s the school had had two rented boarding-houses: Elgin, in the High Street where Martin's garage later stood, and Grove Bank, at the far end of the Grove, opposite St Michael's church. The boys of these, as well as the Head Master, could be accommodated in new houses built in the Hampstead Lane area, and a new chapel could be built there without an Act of Parliament since it would stand on land which was the school's freehold. The whole school would then surround the cricket field, this forming a much larger playground, with the result that discipline could be better maintained because 'the boys could be more easily restrained from going into the Town'.

There were, Ford admitted, three disadvantages: the new site would be less central, it would be 30 ft. lower and therefore less healthy, and the move would be expensive. He dismissed the first two and claimed that the £4,000 which the move would require would 'not be difficult to raise from the school's many friends and old boys'. Dr Dyne, he concluded, 'wished it to be mentioned that the plan suggested in this Memorandum does not originate with him; he will, however, work it out heartily if the Governors as a body determine to take it up.'

The Governors were so far persuaded that they asked the architect, William Butterfield, to prepare plans for the scheme, but when he submitted these the following February he estimated the cost at £19,000. Meanwhile the Governors had also received 'a masterly open letter' from the Revd John Henry Leech, a Fellow of Brasenose who had recently returned to the school to teach the Fifth Form, opposing the scheme. As a result they decided not to pursue it. Less cautious Governors might have saved the school many future problems.

Because of their caution the Parliamentary Commissioners who arrived at Highgate in 1865 found the school still on its ancient and overcrowded site. The last inspection (1818–19) had been carried out by Parliamentary Commissioners investigating schools providing education for the poor. Highgate no longer fitted into that category, nor had it been inspected by the earlier Parliamentary Commissioners of the 1860s, the so-called Clarendon Commission under Lord Clarendon, which had reported on the country's seven most prestigious

The school in 1864. This is the only detailed photograph of the pre-1865 school buildings.

Right: *Elgin House, Highgate High Street, in 1865. Gerard Manley Hopkins was a pupil here until 1863.*

Below: *Poem to celebrate the tercentenary, 1865.*

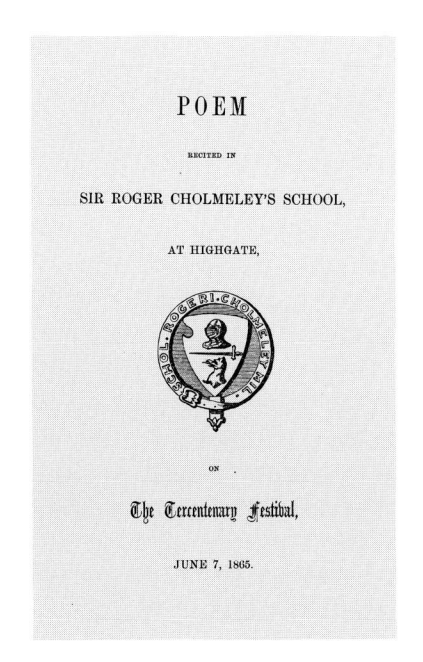

boarding schools (Rugby, Harrow, Winchester, Eton, Shrewsbury, Charterhouse and Westminster) and the two best known day schools (Merchant Taylors' and St Paul's). For comparison it had included appendices on five less well known schools, but these did not include Highgate.

So it was as one of the Endowed Schools, which the Taunton Commission under Lord Taunton was now investigating, that Highgate was visited. Many of the 800 or so schools of this sort which had been founded in Tudor times had foundered, but about 100 survived. The Commissioner who came to Highgate in May 1865, was D. R. Fearon, a man of standing in the educational world, and Dyne did his best to impress him by inviting him to the school's tercentenary celebrations eleven days later.

He was successful. 'The boys', Fearon reported, 'appear to be well taught on the whole, and the standard of education is higher here than at any other school in this district except at the City of London and among the Grecians at Christ's Hospital.' The classics were the central subject studied – all but ten junior boys were learning Greek – and there was still no modern side, but many were receiving at least some education in other subjects: 110 in French, eighty-six in mathematics, sixteen in German, sixteen in drawing. History remained almost entirely Roman, Greek and biblical.

DR DYNE – SECOND FOUNDER

Fearon asked forty boys about the occupations of their parents, and concluded that the school was 'doing very good work for the upper-middle classes'. It was a verdict which was accurate from the start of Dyne's regime, and became increasingly so. Even in his first ten years boys with identifiably upper-middle class parents far outnumbered those from lower-middle class homes. Forty-nine were gentlemen or esquires, no fewer than fifty-two solicitors, barristers or judges, twenty-three clergymen, eighteen in the army or navy, thirteen doctors or surgeons and seven architects. By comparison, three were tradesmen, one each was a coachmaker, baker, grocer, furrier and wax-bleacher and fifteen ambiguously described themselves as merchants. Two years after Dyne left (1875), the only exception in two pages of otherwise exclusively upper-middle class parents was one pig-gelder from 4 Belsize Park, Hampstead.

The Taunton Commission recommended the establishment of a permanent commission to regulate endowed schools. This so alarmed their headmasters that some, led by Thring of Uppingham and Mitchinson of the King's School, Canterbury, prepared to defend themselves. After an initial meeting at the Freemasons' Tavern in London, they held a second at Uppingham, to which Thring claimed that he invited sixty or seventy, but only twelve came. Dyne was one of them (though he did not arrive until the second day). It was this group which formed itself into the Headmasters' Conference. Though the achievements of several other members paralleled Dyne's at Highgate (Thring himself raised his numbers at Uppingham from twenty-five to 320) Dyne's standing among them is suggested by the fact that, for its third meeting in December 1871, the Headmasters' Conference came to Highgate.

A more celebrated visitor than Fearon to the tercentenary celebrations was W. E. Gladstone, Chancellor of the Exchequer. At that afternoon's speech day he

Dr Dyne's slate – used as daily register of attendance, c. 1865–9.

A croquet tournament at Highgate, c. 1870, showing Bishopswood Road houses and the 'old oak' in the background.

Dr Dyne and the Sixth Form, 1869.

his audience that he fervently hoped the school might 'continue to grow in reputation until it is no longer regarded as a local establishment ... but claims its place among those great public schools which are one of the most distinguishing characteristics of England'. The occasion was as much a celebration of Dyne's achievements as of Cholmeley's foundation, and the Head Master was in excellent form. At 8 a.m. he administered Holy Communion at St Michael's, at noon he preached there, at luncheon he toasted the assistant masters and during the rest of the day he made four speeches, three of them at a celebration dinner for old boys and friends. The same year another Gladstone, William, an East India merchant who lived at The Elms, Fitzroy Park, and a Governor since 1863, gave money for the establishment of four scholarships for boarders at the school.

It was also in the tercentenary year that the problem of a chapel was finally solved. Since 1848 the Governors had been considering the matter, their main difficulty the cost. Now, three years after the death of Governor George Abraham Crawley, his family offered the school a chapel in his memory. The two surviving Crawleys most closely involved with the school were his sons, Robert Townsend and George Baden. Both were Old Cholmeleians, both Highgate residents and both were to become Governors. The younger, George, was the better known. 'His adventurous spirit', *The Cholmeleian* wrote, 'prompted him to give up the law, and engage in daring enterprises abroad.' He built railways in Belgium, Spain, Hungary, Romania, Georgia, Venezuela and

Mexico, and the markets of Madrid. On 30 November 1879 he was landing once more at Vera Cruz when a ship's block fell on his head; he died within three hours.

In accepting the Crawleys' gift the Governors insisted that the new chapel should be solely for the use of the school. Outsiders 'could only be admitted by a Governor in person, or by an Order written or verbal of the Head Master'. There was to be no font.

The new chapel in itself would have made a move by the school impossible; furthermore, at the same time the Governors authorised the drawing-up of plans for new school buildings, also on its ancient site.

> [As these] advanced towards completion portions of the old buildings had to be knocked down. Soon we began to be pressed for room, for of course School duties had to be carried on ... Some of the forms had to receive their lessons at Elgin House; some at Grove Bank; and we considered it rather fun to trot about here and there in quest of our various Masters. By the end of the summer term of 1866 the present buildings were finished, and were first used on the last day of term, the Speech Day. In what is now the playground stood on that day the remains of the old buildings – a gaunt shapeless ruin. It was the last I saw of them.

The new chapel, built where the old one had stood, took longer to complete, and was not consecrated until Palm Sunday, 1867.

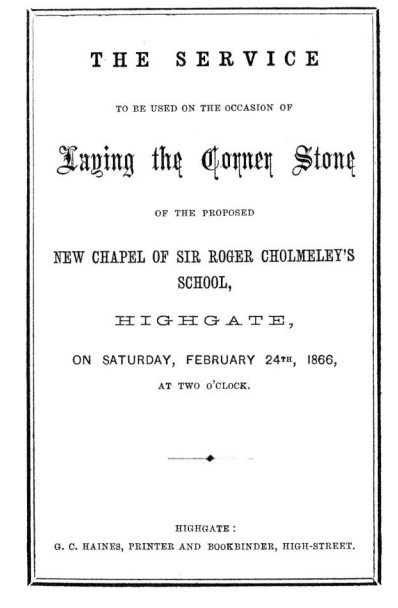

Laying the new chapel corner stone, 24 February 1866.

Pond Square at the heart of the village in the 1860s.

The first issue of The Cholmeleian, *November 1873.*

Though Dyne undoubtedly rescued Highgate, and would later be described by old boys as their 'dear old Master', he was not universally popular. 'He was a desperate "swisher",' Yates wrote. Charles Luxmoore (1858–61) remembered how a boy who was about to be flogged warned Dyne that if he raised his arm above his shoulder he would be summonsed. 'Dyne almost choked with his speechless rage, but at last when he recovered it was hard indeed for the boy.' Until the 1870s almost all the great Victorian headmasters flogged, and not all were disliked for it.

Dyne's treatment of Gerard Manley Hopkins suggests other reasons for his unpopularity. On one occasion Hopkins bet another boy ten shillings to six pence that he would go without all drink for three weeks. Before the end of the period his tongue had turned black.

Such an effort was not done in the corner [Luxmoore wrote]; for three weeks it was the talk of the school, and had the authorities been in touch with their boys ... they had stopped the whole thing at the outset with a few kindly words. My impression is Dyne swooped down on the 22nd day when your brother had won, blustered and threatened, and finally punished both 'betters', compelled Gerard to return the 10s., and bound both by solemn promises and unlimited threats not to pay or receive the bet. In vain your brother pointed out that such a decision really rewarded the other boy, and only punished him who had endured the suffering and exhaustion of the effort. Dyne was obdurate and Gerard ... only heaped up to himself further punishment ... A Headmaster less heavy-handed and headed than Dyne would have appreciated the value of such a boy, and kept him ever on his side, but blustering Dyne's argument was always 'hold your tongue, Sir', his firm conviction that a boy must be always wrong, and his appeal never to reason, always to force.

A contemporary engraving showing the new school buildings, 1867.

Hopkins, according to Luxmoore, 'was a quiet, gentle, upright boy ... there was no fight in him, unless he was unjustly used or attacked, and in that he was godlike, for it sprang from his love of justice, of truth.' Hopkins himself described how he was deprived of the room he had been given in which to work for an exhibition

> for the most trifling little thing ... Dyne and I had a terrific altercation. I was driven out of patience and cheeked him wildly, and he blazed into me with his riding-whip ... Shortly after ... like a fool I seized one of the upstairs candles on Sunday night when they had taken ours away too soon and my room was denied me for a week ... Before, however, it was time for me to resume possession I was in a worse row than ever about absolutely nothing ... Clarke, my co-victim, was flogged, struck off the confirmation list and fined £1; I was deprived of my room for ever, sent to bed at half-past nine till further orders, and ordered to work *only* in the school room, not even in the school library.

Dyne, Hopkins added, 'had repeatedly said he hoped I might not be at the top of the school after the exam., so you may suppose, when he took these last measures, I drew my own conclusion.' If this was Dyne's intention the external examiner from Brasenose frustrated it. On 16 April 1862 he told the Governors, 'I have examined this school and more especially five boys who were mentioned to me as Candidates for the Exhibition. Of these ... Hopkins, Beaumont, Tatham and Richardson were not far distant from each other; and between the two first-named I found such a near approach to equality as to make the decision very difficult. On a careful review of their work, however, I find myself able to decide in favour of Hopkins.'

There is one more mention of Hopkins in the Governors' minute book; five years later Governors Ford and Tatham reported that 'they were of opinion that Mr Hopkins had not forfeited his Exhibition by becoming a Roman Catholic'. When, however, Hopkins died of typhoid at the age of 45, *The Cholmeleian's* obituary described his conversion as 'the crisis of his life ... which parted him from us'.

During his last five years Dyne continued to be generous to the school. In 1869 he, together with Governor Bloxham, lent it £5,000 out of £7,000 needed to buy more playing-fields in Hampstead Lane. And he and Governor Ford each contributed £25 out of £81 spent on altering the chapel's seats to make kneeling more comfortable.

On 28 August 1873 he wrote to Governor Bloxham offering his resignation. 'It will be evident to all the Governors that the time has come when I require a somewhat less busy and anxious life than a School affords'. The following 30 March the school chapel, according to *The Cholmeleian*, 'witnessed a larger gathering than has met within its walls since its consecration'. Those who had come, 'naturally wished to hear the parting words of one who, by his influence and unwearied energy for thirty-five years, had raised the School from obscurity to its present position'.

In his parting words Dyne described the school's senior boys as 'the salt of

Engraving showing Dodd's forge on the High Street and the new school chapel in the background, mid-nineteenth century.

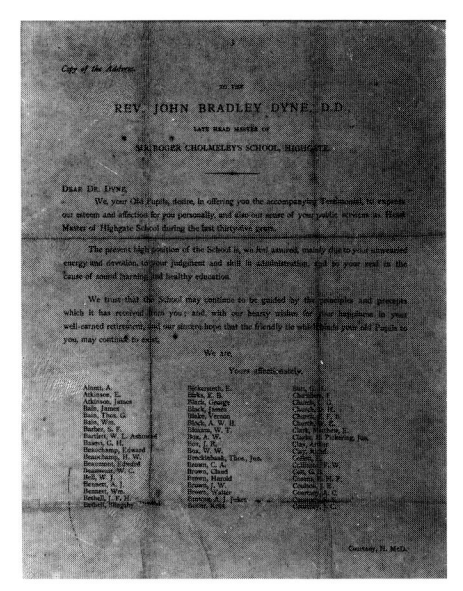

Right: *Dr Dyne and his staff, 1872. Left to right: A. R. de Beaumont, Revd R. L. Morris, W. C. Wood, Dr Dyne, Revd R. Fletcher, Revd W. D. Bodkin, Revd W. H. Elton, and E. L. Roy.*

Above: *Testimonial to Dyne from former pupils on his 35th year at Highgate, and his retirement.*

the earth; and if the salt hath lost its savour, wherewith shall it be salted'. The Preacher, *The Cholmeleian* noted, 'was visibly affected'. Next day Dyne was presented with a silver ink-stand by the boys of the school; the assistant masters had already given him 'a handsome reading-lamp', and the Old Cholmeleians gave him a handsome clock, an illuminated address and a purse of £400. Less generously, the Governors decided that they could not afford him a pension – but perhaps he did not need one. Fearon had estimated that, apart from his £400 salary, £25 coal allowance and free house, he had been earning £1,000 to £1,200 a year from his boarders – this at a time when the salary of an average assistant master was £150. (By comparison, a doctor in general practice at this time could expect after eight or ten years to be earning not less than £500 a year.)

Dyne lived on for another quarter of a century, dying in December 1898. Meanwhile, in 1882 his identically named son had become a Governor.

5

SUCCEEDING AN INSTITUTION
1874–1893

THERE WERE TWENTY-SIX candidates for the position of Dyne's successor. After various interviews the Governors unanimously chose Charles McDowall. Like Dyne, McDowall was in holy orders (all candidates had to be) and was to become a Doctor of Divinity, but unlike Dyne when appointed, he was already an experienced schoolmaster. He had taught first at Rossall, the north-country school which gave reduced fees to sons of the clergy, then at Malvern where he had become Second Master. And while Dyne was short, slight and clean-shaven, McDowall was tall, massive and enormously bearded.

It was hardly surprising that he found the school seriously in need of modernising. While Dyne had retained the classics as the only subject taught seriously, other well-known schools had been establishing modern sides, probably the first of them McDowall's old school, Rossall. That year (1854) Marlborough did the same and others followed, Clifton from its foundation in 1862, Haileybury by 1863, Wellington in 1867 and Charterhouse in 1872. The start of science teaching had sometimes coincided, but sometimes followed only later; at Marlborough, for example, not until 1871 when Farrar (author of *Eric or Little by Little* and an improbable enthusiast for science) poached Clifton's science master. Farrar's lecture to the Royal Institution in 1868 had included a particularly violent attack on the classics, both the way they were taught and the way they dominated the curriculum at most public schools.

Inspired without doubt by such events and opinions, McDowall had within six months abolished such relics of earlier times as compulsory Greek Testament every Saturday for upper forms. By his first autumn term he had established a modern side, and introduced science. If in doing this he was not ahead of all other schools, some of the best known had still to follow – Shrewsbury, Westminster, Eton and Winchester, for example.

The bell gate on North Road in the 1870s. The gate is the oldest feature of the school that is still recognisable today.

Three years later (February 1877) McDowall reported to the Governors on his achievements so far. The number of boys had risen from about 160 to 208; there were now fourteen assistant masters; 'the range of Education' had been 'materially widened by greater attention to Modern Languages and Drawing, and by the introduction of the study of Natural Science'. Boys were now 'passing such examinations as that of the London University Matriculation (in which a knowledge of Chemistry and Natural Science is required), the Army, Civil Service etc., with no further tuition than that which they receive at the school'. This was a time when boys from public schools regularly had to leave early and go to a crammer or private tutor to pass such exams.

McDowell appended a list of his assistant masters. There were still two who taught nothing but the classics and five who taught classics as well as mathematics, but there were also two drawing masters, one singing master, a chemistry master, a French master and one who also taught some German. The French master was A. R. de Beaumont, described as 'late French Tutor to

H. R. H. Prince Arthur'. In employing a Frenchman, Highgate was also ahead of many contemporaries. As late as 1890 Canon Bell of Marlborough told an interviewer, 'I so much believe in discipline that I have no foreign masters at all. All French and German is taught, and thoroughly, although not colloquially, by Englishmen.' In his twenty-two years at Highgate, de Beaumont became a notable school eccentric; 5 ft. 3 in. tall, 'majestic, white-whiskered', he was believed to have been head of the horse-dealing department of the French Army. 'His little vanities were all connected with his desire to shine as an adopted Englishman. Once or twice a year he was to be seen walking up and down outside his house in Hampstead Lane at an early hour in the evening, with his coat open to show his evening clothes. The parade lasted for some time and was intended to provoke enquiry. Asked where he was going, he would answer shortly, but with dignity, "I am going to dine at ze Guards' Mess" ... He would deal out ferocious impositions' but 'withdraw them on the thinnest pretext', and was famous for the order 'The 'ole class will go to ze bottom'. When de Beaumont fell ill and retired, 250 boys and masters contributed to a fund which not only paid his medical expenses but provided him (or his wife) with a £40 annuity for their lives.

Monsieur A. R. de Beaumont, staff 1870–92, a refugee after the Franco-Prussian war.

The teaching of science (and singing) remained a problem, McDowall's report continued, because of the lack of 'a detached lecture-room ... at a little distance from the other buildings. This want will be supplied by the acquisition of the British School, and I would press the necessity of obtaining possession of it at

Revd Charles McDowall, Head Master 1874–93.

the earliest opportunity.' He and the Treasurer had already visited the British School, an oddly shaped building, 30 ft. high, 60 ft. long, 38 ft. wide at one end and 20 ft. wide at the other, which stood farther along Southwood Lane. Now the Treasurer recommended the acceptance of the asking price (£1,200) in case there was a rival offer. In July the Charity Commissioners gave their approval, and the British School was duly bought and converted into upper and lower laboratories and two more classrooms.

McDowall had an equally urgent request. 'If the highest tone and character is to be given to the School, if, in face of keen competition and the improved accommodation of other schools, ours is to hold its place, a well adapted boarding house in the Head Master's hands is absolutely indispensable.' He already kept a number of boarders, as Dyne had done, at his own house, but what he now wanted was the sort of house becoming usual at other schools, for about sixty boys. He was entitled to feel impatient. When his job had been advertised the Head Master's rewards had included 'any profits to be received from a boarding house which the Head Master will have the opportunity of renting'.

The delay had been caused by arguments lasting seven years between the Governors and, first, the Endowed Schools Commission, then the Charity Commissioners, about new statutes for the school. These were finally approved by the Queen in Council on 12 August 1876. The boys of the school, McDowall assured them, would not notice much change. Nevertheless, they made important new provisions, one being that in future there should be six more Governors, nominated one each by the Lord Lieutenant of Middlesex, the Bishop of London, the Lord Chief Justice and the Universities of Oxford, Cambridge and London. Another was that, in place of the original forty free scholars, the Governors would be allowed to 'grant exemptions', total or partial of tuition fees for such periods ... as they saw fit' to boys they might choose, who were to be known as Foundation Scholars. The number of these was not to exceed 10 per cent of the school (except with permission of the Charity Commissioners).

Meanwhile McDowall's boarding house, for which plans had first been prepared as early as June 1874, remained unstarted; in December 1876 the new Governors postponed its building for another six months, so that they should 'have an opportunity of more fully acquainting themselves with the educational requirements and financial position of the School'. At last, however, it was begun, and in January 1881 School House finally opened. According to *The Cholmeleian* it could take between forty and fifty boys, and was 'acknowledged to be one of the finest and most completely fitted in the kindgom'.

The new house made possible an equally important development: the founding of a Junior School. For its building this used the old Head Master's house in Southwood Lane. This was renamed Cholmeley House, and junior boarders were transferred there from other boarding houses. Soon afterwards Northfield Hall was acquired as a gymnasium. In 1884 a sanatorium was built at 87 Southwood Lane and in 1885 a swimming-bath at one side of the Senior Field (boys had previously swum in the pool at Ken Wood). Eleven years later the new pool was boarded over in winter to replace Northfield Hall as a gymnasium.

It was also during McDowall's time that various extra-curricular activities and

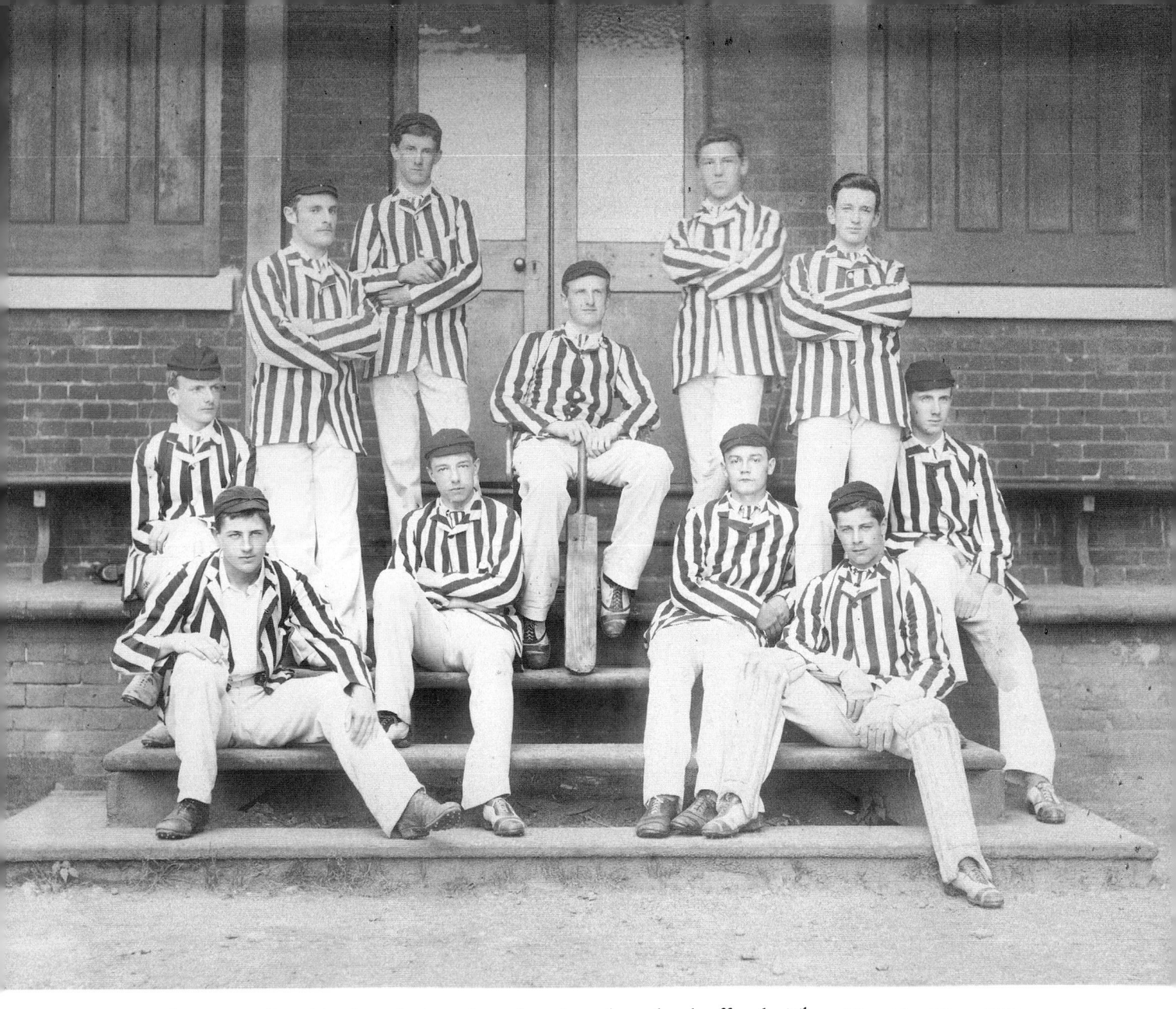

The cricket XI, c. 1890.

societies began to flourish, broadening the education the school offered. *The Cholmeleian* had been launched the year before he arrived. 'The want of a periodical', it first leader admitted, 'has been all the more felt, since almost every other school of any importance is thus represented.' Like other school magazines, it gave much space to games; unlike some, it also printed poetry, short stories and articles. The boys of the school seem to have taken a particular interest in foreign travel. Between October 1874 and October 1876 articles included 'The Festival of the Prophet at Cairo', 'A Flying Visit to Canada', 'Into and Out of Nubia', 'A "P. & O." Breakdown', 'A Voyage to the South Sea Islands', and 'How We saw the Isle of Wight'.

Besides cricket and football matches, it reported that traditional Highgate sport, the paper-chase. These were staged on Michaelmas Day (29 September) and Shrove Tuesday. At 2.15 p.m. on Michaelmas Day 1873 the hares (assistant masters Ford and Bodkin) arrived at the cricket field gates with their bags full of paper slung over their shoulders. At 2.30 they set off down Bishopswood Road, the hounds following nine minutes later as far as the entrance into Baker's

Christmas concert, 1885. The programme included music by Mendelssohn and songs with librettos by Shakespeare, Coleridge and Shelley.

fields. Here 'with the cry of "Tally Ho!" we rushed through a prickly hedge, and entered upon our chase across country towards Finchley. After crossing about two fields we were checked for a moment by a hedge with a ditch on the other side, forming a drop of about ten feet, but only for a moment. Over flew the two foremost hounds almost simultaneously, and indeed too simultaneously, for one dropped to the ground on top of the other, and they both rolled over in ... no very gentle embrace.'

From Finchley the trail led through Totteridge then along 'the very same track we followed last year, which had brought us to High Barnet, and took us through the very field in which, last year, our course was checked for a few minutes by two brawny sons of the sod, armed with pitchforks.' The hares were eventually found at an inn on the Great North Road.

Early *Cholmeleians* also reported the activities of the school's new societies. The Natural History Society met regularly to listen to papers on such diverse subjects as a recent meteorite (Revd William Bodkin), and Mummies (Mr Eugene Roy). But the great event of its year was its Conversazione, held on some evening towards the end of the Christmas term. The first of these (18 December 1873) was attended by 300 members and guests.

> The Library was thrown open, and in it was placed, among other objects of interest, a cabinet of butterflies, lent by members of the Society ... The School Choir, under the direction of Mr H. J. Lawner, sang various glees, which greatly tended to the enjoyment of the evening – viz., 'Glorious Apollo', 'Hail Smiling Morn', 'Golden slumber kiss thine eyes', ... 'See, our oars with feathered spray' ... The first address was by Mr E. Fry QC, the subject being 'Volcanoes in Central France' ... The Conversazione was closed, about eleven o'clock, with the National Anthem.

Like other school natural history societies of the nineteenth century, Highgate's considered that amateurs, in the tradition of Gilbert White, could make important contributions to science. It urged members not to regard its meetings merely as a way to while away an hour or so every fortnight, but to go out into the countryside, record observations and collect specimens. In November 1875 it passed a motion that 'two-thirds of the funds of the Society be devoted to scientific purposes'.

In the same years the Debating Society began to hold regular meetings. At the earliest reported by *The Cholmeleian* a boy, E. H. R. Tatham, proposed 'That the character of Queen Elizabeth is worthy of the highest admiration', and was unsuccessfully opposed by the Revd William Bodkin. The Society was not large. On 2 December 1875 the motion, 'That this House sympathizes with the Insurgents in Herzegovina' was carried by seven votes to five. Other early motions seem strangely familiar: 'That the abolition of the House of Lords would impair the balance of the British Constitution' (carried seven to one); 'That the mental capacities of women were fully equal to those of men' (carried seven to three); 'That the proposed Channel Tunnel, from many points of view, is a most undesirable scheme' (no vote reported, but 'one of the best debates that have taken place for a long while, showing that though the number of debates were few, yet it was more owing to increased interest in the sports and the fine weather, than to any decline of interest in the society'). Other motions were topical: 'That a system of compulsory army service might be introduced into this country, and would be beneficial to the nation' (lost by six votes). Highgate's boys were apparently less worried than the country's politicians by the great conscript armies of France and Germany.

A few years later came a Science Society, at which audiences as large as fifty heard lectures on such basic subjects as Heat. (What, one wonders, were they being taught in their science classes?) In the winter term of 1889 the (revived) Science Society became the Lecture Society. Meanwhile, in 1877, the collapsed Shakespeare Reading Society was refounded as the Literary Society; at its first two meetings it read *The Merchant of Venice* and *King Lear*. Its episodic life continued. Refounded again in 1883, it read *Much Ado about Nothing*, then, leaping boldly foward a century and a half, *School for Scandal*. At its next revival (1889) it was positively adventurous, starting with *The Overland Route* by the contemporary playwright, Tom Taylor.

The keenest supporter of many of these early societies was the Revd William Bodkin, a man equally willing to lead a paper-chase or lecture on the attention given to her eggs by his pet tortoise. For some years he was housemaster of Grove Bank, but in December 1884 his old college, King's, Cambridge, offered him the comfortable living of Ringwood, Hampshire, where he was the vicar for the next thirty-two years.

By the 1870s organised games were a well-established feature of the school,

The opening of the Highgate Cable Tramway in 1884. Horse trams could not easily climb Highgate Hill. The cable tramway – the first in Europe – hauled trams up on a continuous moving wire. Technical difficulties and accidents dogged the tramway until its demise in 1909.

The 1885 football team, earliest existing photograph of a soccer team at the school.

if less of an obsession than at most purely boarding schools. The main opponents at cricket were Merchant Taylors' School and St Paul's, at Rugby football, Merchant Taylors' and Dulwich College. In September 1878, however, the school's football was traumatically disrupted when McDowall, probably because of recent injuries in Rugby games, announced that Association football should be played instead. *The Cholmeleian* was loyally uncritical, but felt it necessary to give some basic advice about the new game. 'It should, we repeat, be borne in mind by all that to dribble the ball a yard at a time and back it up closely behind is the only way to do real service, and that to kick it where there is not a chance of following it up is worse than useless.'

Highgate's Corps was not one of the earliest. In 1860 a number of school Corps had been founded, in response to Palmerston's appeal for a Volunteer force to repel a threatened French invasion. Soon afterwards there was a Highgate village Volunteer unit, attached to the 14th Middlesex Rifle Volunteers. In

March 1866 this unit asked the Governors to renew its lease of a building in Southwood Lane, but otherwise it was not connected with the school, and only in 1891 was there an agitation among the boys for a school Volunteer Corps. This led to a meeting between boys of upper forms and the Head Master, after which McDowall circulated parents and then, on one of the last days of the winter term, announced that the unit would be formed.

It was attached to the 3rd Middlesex Rifle Volunteers, and in its early days was much helped by that unit's commander, Lt. Col. Hennell DSO. For a while, like most newly formed military units, it lacked almost everything except enthusiasm. At 12.30 on 2 February 1892 its two squads, numbering in total almost sixty, began to drill 'in earnest'. Captain J. G. Lamb, described as 'a schoolmaster who should have been a soldier', took charge, and at first ordered four drills a week because there was 'so much to be learned'. Boys over 17 received the government grant for drill and class-firing.

After a two-month wait, 100 Martini Henry rifles arrived. Uniform took longer, and the Corps was not properly dressed until the end of May 1892. Its members wore a grey Norfolk jacket (Middlesex Regiment colours), helmet and leggings, with a rolled greatcoat attached to the waist-belt. By this time it also had rifles fitted with Morris Tubes (to reduce the bore to take .22 rounds for short-range practice) and had begun to use a range at the back of Northfield Hall. It had also taken part in a minor operation on Parliament Hill. At its first inspection on 3 June, fifty-eight members paraded, including a bugler. In September it went by train for a field day to Hitchen, where, together with Haileybury's Corps, it attacked a position held by the Hitchen and Royston Volunteers. The result was judged a success, though one Highgate section pursued the enemy cyclists and was 'not to be found for some time'. At the 1892 Speech Day the Head Master described the founding of the Corps as the great

The Highgate Volunteer Corps in its first year, July 1892.

event of the year. A year and a half later in February 1894 the Corps was under the command of Lt. Hetherington, on account of 'the absence of Captain Lamb, who is still, we regret to say, laid up with a protracted attack of gout'. It survived this early casualty to become an established part of school life.

In the last months of McDowall's regime a number of the school's old boys began to campaign for the founding of an association. They felt that, although Old Cholmeleians had dined together for over thirty years (since 1859), something more formal was needed. In the spring of 1893 they announced the founding of a club, and Franklyn Lushington, member of a well-known Highgate School family, became its secretary.

The club met for the first time the following December, the date chosen 'to enable all those who might attend the O.C. match against the school to attend'. Seventy of them did so. They set up an Entertainments Committee to arrange dinners, as well as cricket, football and fives sections. The club's main purpose was to maintain contact between the school and its old boys, in particular by encouraging them to attend school functions. All members of the club – about 100 at first – would receive *The Cholmeleian.*

The club's first dinner was held the following 7 April, Sports Day. Sixty members came, and interspersed their speeches with song. 'G. R. Crawford Esq. voiced a deep-tongued "Private Tommy Atkins", the Revd H. A. P. Sawyer warbled naïvely about his "Sally in our Alley", the Secretary chanted "The Yeoman's Wedding" song.' In the years ahead membership steadily increased, reaching 631 by 1919, and almost 4,000 by 1968. That year the Society, as it renamed itself in 1916, acquired its own room in Dyne House (newly built on the site of Cholmeley House) where the school's first Record Keeper, Theodore Mallinson, has collected its excellent archives.

Highgate School never received a more severe shock than it did on 29 June 1893 when the Revd Charles McDowall, its Head Master by then for nineteen years but still only 56, collapsed and died. 'Until within fifteen minutes of his death,' *The Times* reported, 'he was apparently in the best of health. While watching the boys at cricket he said he felt ill, and would go into the house. He sat down, and before Mrs McDowall could send for assistance was dead.' 'The blow which has fallen on us with terrible suddenness,' *The Cholmeleian* began its black-edged editorial. Next day at an emergency meeting the Governors put the Revd Sandford Simons, a Cambridge mathematician, in charge, and though they decided that the school should remain open, they cancelled Speech Day. On the day of McDowall's funeral, according to the *Hampstead and Highgate Express*, 'The blinds of nearly every private house of Highgate were drawn ... and all the shops were partially closed.'

McDowall, in the words of C. A. Evors (a master he appointed in 1885 who published a 1938 history of the school) was 'the personification of dignity; shy and reserved until you broke through his defence. Then charming.' He would often be seen cantering about Hampstead Heath, attended by his groom. He had proved a worthy successor to Dyne, modernising the school in ways which Dyne was too much of a traditionalist to attempt. Under McDowall Highgate came close to transforming itself into one of the country's great boarding schools.

Black-bordered obituary in The Cholmeleian *after McDowell's sudden death.*

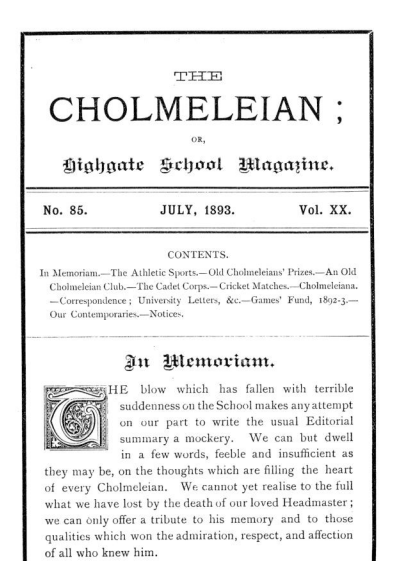

6

ALLCOCK – DEAR OLD BOY
1893–1908

LIKE HIS PREDECESSOR, the Revd Arthur Edmund Allcock, who became Head Master for the autumn term of 1893, was an experienced teacher, but unlike either McDowall or Dyne, both of whom were classicists, he was a mathematician. For the previous thirteen years he had taught at Wellington, the last seven in charge of its Army Class. None of this, nor his portrait with sad, drooping moustache, painted the year before he died, suggests that he was also a fanatical games player, who listed his recreations in *Who's Who* as cricket, fives and golf.

Allcock apparently discovered that all was not well at the school he had inherited. 'He at once showed himself a strong man by the way in which he handled certain perplexing and unpleasant problems', Evors wrote. Whatever it was that Evors referred to, he hurried on to a less delicate subject: Allcock's organisation of the day boys (still more than half the school's 274) into houses. In this he was following the example of a school like Clifton, which also had a significant number of day boys. Evors himself became one of the new housemasters, Lamb another. The result was of particular benefit to the school's games. Now there could be competitions in which the new day boy houses together with the boarding houses, School House and Fitzroy Lodge (Grove Bank and Elgin had been closed) could all take part.

It was a period when games were considered at least as important as work. Walter Kay (1904–8) remembered a summer morning when he was taking a paper for the Maths prize which he hoped to win. Suddenly a master arrived, tapped him on the shoulder and said 'Kay, the MCC have turned up with twelve men; you're wanted to go and make twelfth man for the school.' Though Kay deplored the incident, his most vivid memory of school was of this match, in which he earned his school colours, while Philip Taylor's (1901–6) was of the game in which he took all ten wickets in an innings. Allcock was certainly not

Revd Arthur Edmund Allcock, Head Master 1893–1908.

Highgate School, 1894.

a man to demote athleticism, indeed he improved the school's games facilities, building the six fives courts which survive today beside the Senior Field, and ejecting allotment holders from school land in Bishopswood Road to create the Junior Field. In the holidays, a bachelor, he would invite parties of boys to his Aberdovey home, where he would teach them golf.

Highgate was saved from the total obsession with games which gripped so many public schools from the 1860s until at least the start of the Second World War by its day boys. For them games were not compulsory and many played none. Two letters to *The Cholmeleian* of December 1895 suggest the balance of attitudes to games in the school.

Cricket team, c. 1895.

Sir, I wish to utter a protest against the unpatriotic behaviour of the unsportsmanlike portion of the school. Surely there is nothing to prevent fellows who do not play games from coming down to the field, when there are matches in progress, and cheering on their representatives ... At a large number of public schools, attendance in the field is compulsory.
Yours very sincerely, A. E. Burnie [Captain of Cricket].

Sir, As one of those day boys, who are such a great ornament to the School, although they do not play games, I would like to answer some of the accusations made against us ... I think that a fellow with any sense in his head would admit that it is the wisest course we could pursue. It would be lowering to our dignity to take part in such vulgar games. Besides, crowning reason, we do not know where the field is.

I am yours truly, Day Boy.

The Cholmeleian appealed for an answer to 'so palpable a trifler', but if one came it was never published.

Allcock's enthusiasm for games did not prevent him being liked and admired by boys of all sorts, nor from taking a serious interest in the school's work, especially its mathematics. He would visit maths classes where, Kay remembered, he would ask the boys if they had problems: 'And of course ... we all knew the questions we wanted to ask, because ... he was ambidextrous; he could go up to a blackboard with a piece of chalk in his [right] hand, and draw a perfect circle. Nothing very much in that, but we all knew what was coming. He would rub that one out to put up another picture, and ... he'd walk up quite naturally with the chalk in his left hand and draw a perfect circle. The boys all knew this; it shows you the sort of rapport there was between the boys and the masters.' To Kay he was 'a dear old boy'. Taylor remembered that 'he was delightful, very scholarly, very quiet ... You never got to know him well; you always had very great respect for him.'

Just the same, the academic standards of Highgate in Allcock's time were adequate rather than outstanding. An average boy like Frank Adey (1906–8)

Below left: *Shooting VIII, 1897.*

Below: *Big School, c. 1895. The pump below the sundial today stands in the chapel cloister.*

considered that he was worked hard, with homework in the evening which he couldn't do in less than three hours. 'Being partly a boarding school, I suppose they had to do something with the chaps in the evening.' But a clever boy like Kay remembered that 'I never really bothered about homework at all ... it was all stuff I knew very well.'

The school was now organised into three bottom classes, taught in three classrooms below Big School ('the Dungeons'), then on the classical side into the Remove, the Shell, the Fifth and Sixth Forms, and on the modern side into the Lower, Middle and Upper Forms. Life in the modern Upper Form was especially relaxed. Work wasn't marked so boys 'didn't have to do everything. You did it if you felt like it' (Kay).

Allcock's most important contribution to Highgate was to its premises: Central Hall, and the classroom block below today's Dyne House. In September 1895 he told the Governors that the school's buildings were 'not in accordance with the requirements of the present day'. A subcommittee of Governors agreed. At St Paul's (which they visited) they noted in particular a dining hall for day boys, one of the items the Head Master was asking for. Others were more classrooms, better provision for the teaching of physics, chemistry and drawing,

Revd A. E. Allcock and School House, 1890s.

Annual inspection of the OTC, 1897, in only its fifth year. School House is in the background.

There were two problems. The school would have to borrow to build. When McDowall had unsuccessfully made a similar request in 1882 it had been over £28,000 in debt and it still owed £14,000. And part of the suggested site was now occupied by fives courts, two temporary classrooms and two cottages. Loss of rent on these, together with interest on extra borrowing and a sinking fund which the Charity Commissioners required would cost over £800 a year. On the other hand the fees of just forty-three extra boys would cover this, and 'such an increase might be reasonably expected'. Despite the risk the Governors engaged an architect, C. P. Leach (an Old Cholmeleian, son of a Governor, known in his day for inventing a bomb-throwing catapult) to draw up a plan which they presently accepted.

During 1898 and the early months of 1899 the boys watched the new building gradually rise above the stockade which surrounded it, until this was finally removed in time for a ceremonial opening by the Bishop of London on Speech Day, 25 July 1899. Reporting the event, *The Cholmeleian* noted that 'the spacious, well-lighted hall and gallery excited well-deserved admiration'. More cautiously it continued, 'the heating apparatus is highly ornamental, and we may hope to find it useful'.

The main feature of Leach's building – its hall with surrounding gallery, rising to lantern roof – remains little changed today. The rooms which surrounded it on ground and first floor originally made nine classrooms, a study for the Head Master, a staff Common Room, a drawing studio and a large dining-hall for day boys. Since then they have been put to many different uses. The new classroom block behind and below the then Junior School (Dyne's old house, renamed Cholmeley House) followed a few years later, and was formally opened in June 1904. This, too, survives much as originally built.

Meanwhile bad news had steadily been reaching Britain about the Boer War, and when at last there was good news the school, like the rest of the country, celebrated.

> In the dead of night a band of patriots, intoxicated with joy and other things, roused every house in the town with the news that Mafeking and its brave defenders are saved. The School met as usual ... but it did not disperse as usual. At 9.45 about a hundred boys charged down North Road, carried by storm an unfortified and scantily garrisoned flag shop, and proceeded to parade the town with the captured standards of the enemy. The leaders of the procession tried to raise the National Anthem or a patriotic chorus, but their attempts were drowned in the cheers of their followers, which reached a climax whenever a stray master was sighted crossing the track; it was only when the antics of two skittish cart-horses caused a moment's lull in the shouting that 'God save the Queen' was allowed to have its way. The proceedings ended with a march on the School House, where in a few moments the sacred precincts of the Head Master's front door were in a state of siege and bombardment. The position, which was a strong one, was turned by a flanking movement through the Boys' Entrance, and the Head Master himself appeared on the door steps. His cordial and patriotic speech was received with three hearty cheers, and, after one desperate attempt to croak 'He's a jolly good fellow' with voices already cracked, the crowd dispersed. During the rest of the day the celebrations continued ... we hear that Fitzroy Lodge had a Mafeking tea and champagne supper.

Meanwhile in South Africa many Old Cholmeleians were serving. They included Trooper Lionel Rawson (1886–92) who on 16 May 1900, wrote home,

> After leaving our horses we got into a dried up donga, which we followed down until we got within 500 yards of the river. Here we extended across the plain, and got within about 300 yards of the bushes on the bank of the river, when they opened a perfect fusilade upon us. We immediately dropped flat on the plain, and lay there with no shelter at all for three mortal hours, never moving a foot. They were firing on us from both flanks and in front, and the bullets simply fell like hailstones. I have come to the conclusion that, taken all round, the Boers are simply rotten shots, or we should all have been killed. The brutes were using ... explosive bullets, and they would strike the ground perhaps within a foot of you and go off like a stock whip. I must say I was in a blue funk for the first hour, but you get accustomed to it, and towards the last we were quite callous, some even sleeping where they lay.

Rawson survived the Boer War but was killed in action in December 1916.

In the December 1900 issue of *The Cholmeleian* Trooper Charles Perks (1885–91) described the behaviour of public school boys like himself who were serving in the ranks. 'P[ublic] S[chool] T[ommy] Atkins Esq. has a great opinion of the wisdom he imbibed in school days, and very boldly criticises

Etchings by E. Burrow, 1899, showing (above) the old oak and (below) the baths and the old fountain on the Senior Field, Bishopswood Road.

everything ... He ... likes to do everything in his own time and fashion, but when, as sometimes happens, he figures in a somewhat scathing criticism, he is quite astonished, and can't make it out at all ... With brother Atkins we generally hit it off very amicably, though we often come in for a little "chaff". One elegant trooper, who still sports his eyeglass, gives a great chance for the display of facetiousness.'

By May 1900, 100 Cholmeleians were serving in the imperial army, twenty-five of them in South Africa. When the war ended four had lost their lives in it.

Early in Allcock's time (March 1894) masters and Sixth Form boys met to discuss the formation of a school mission. This was not the first time Highgate had supported missionary work. It had helped a Delhi mission, where the Revd Edward Bickersteth, oldest of five brothers who had been at the school in the 1860s and 70s, was working. When Bickersteth became Bishop of Japan, it sent contributions there, but the boys never showed much interest in converting the Japanese, and now the Revd S. B. Simons, the master who had taken temporary charge when McDowall died, suggested a mission 'as near Highgate as possible'.

By this time a number of other schools had decided that the English working classes were in as much need of Christian support as foreign natives; Winchester established an English mission in 1876, Eton soon afterwards, Marlborough in 1881. Often a school chose a parish where an old boy was the Minister, and Highgate did this when it selected Whitechapel, where the Revd Ernest Sanders (1871–7) was Rector. The school decided to support a curate there and to promote a Boys' Brigade, which would have cricket and football clubs, a debating society, a library and a drum and fife band.

Missions like Highgate's were valuable to boys of the school in a way foreign missions had never been, introducing them to a class of fellow countrymen they

Prayers for the end of the Boer War.

The north end of Big School when it was being used as the library, c. 1900.

rarely met. Soon boys (and masters) were going regularly to Whitechapel in the evening where they taught the eighty members of the mission club to play chess, draughts and bagatelle, and provided them with a vaulting horse and 'a liberal supply of boxing gloves'. In October 1895 the school gave its first concert there, Miss Crich (pronounced Cry-ch, matron of School House) accompanying the soloists on the piano.

In February next year, at newly opened premises in Leman Street, the new music director, Francis Cunningham Woods, 'besides giving us inimitable renderings of "Twanky Diho" ... and "The Presbyterian Cat", undertook all the accompaniments, coached us in the Plantation Song, and infused his own enthusiasm into the whole entertainment.' By then, however, Sanders had moved to Dalston, and in 1897, partly for this reason, partly because of the inaccessibility of Whitechapel, partly 'owing to the influx of Jews into the parish', the mission also moved to Dalston.

Here a Lads' Brigade was formed, and the mission soon congratulated itself on 'supplying something which was totally non-existent before we went to Dalston'. It functioned four times a week as follows:

Sunday   Bible Class, from 3 to 4 p.m. in the church
Monday   Social Evening, from 7.30 to 9 p.m. in the Mission Rooms
Wednesday   Drill, from 7.45 to 9 p.m. in the Lecture Hall
Friday   Social Evening, from 7.30 to 9.30 p.m. at the Mission Rooms.

By 1899 the visit of the lads of the brigade to Highgate to 'enjoy the hospitality of the Head Master' had become the club's 'great event of the season'. The Boys' Club as it is now known) still operates in Dalston and is still supported by the school. The link between Highgate and Dalston is celebrated in the annual

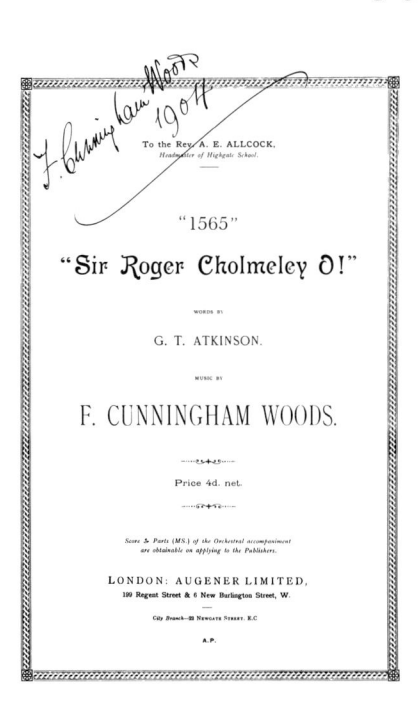

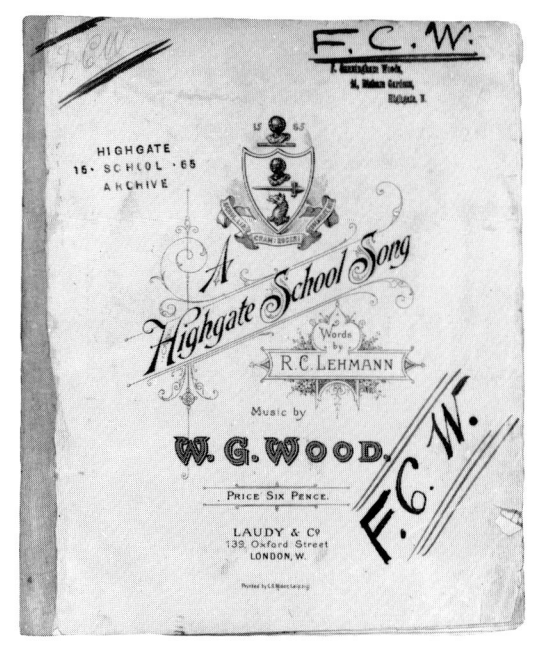

Far right: *Francis Cunningham Woods' copy of the school song of c. 1900, with words by R.C. Lehmann, Old Cholmeleian and later editor of Punch.*

Right: *A copy of 'Sir Roger Cholmeley O!' signed by Cunningham Woods.*

Cricketing scenes in c. 1905, from the album of C. R. Walker who joined the school in 1903.

carol service at St Mark's Dalston, sung by the school's chapel choir.

The appointment of Cunningham Woods as the director of music had been a consequence of the sudden death from acute laryngitis in September 1895 of his predecessor, William George Wood. (To add confusion to the similarity of their names, Woods was known by the boys as 'Highgate Wood'.) William Wood in his nine years at the school had done much for its music, arranging successful concerts every Christmas and improving the singing of the choir. He was a fine organist and has perhaps unfairly been eclipsed by his successor. Cunningham Woods held the position for thirty-four years. As the description of his performance at the mission concert of 1896 suggests, he was an ebullient character, who had been 'in request' at Oxford 'for his comic turns'. His talent as a comic made him seem to some 'more or less a joke, and almost there for the boys' entertainment', but most of them recognised him as a musician of quality. He is remembered for setting eight of the school's songs to music, but he made a more important contribution to school life by starting the orchestra and creating a general enthusiasm for music making.

Boys of Allcock's time remember above all that Highgate was a happy school, to which they were proud to belong. Kay and his friends would wear their half-blue, half-red caps with school badges at home in the holidays. True, there was corporal punishment, but less than at most schools of the time. Taylor remembered being beaten only once ('It was in the morning and I hadn't done my duty'). When he became a prefect he decided that he didn't want to beat. Masters gave lines. Charles Marriott, 'a great rugger player ... a great big chap', would amuse himself while his class did Latin translation by aiming paper pellets at the gap at the top of his classroom window. 'You can imagine the class watching; but if he caught anybody watching he'd get 25 lines straight off.' Marriott, however, also gave credit for good work or behaviour. '"Let that boy off the next 25 lines I gave him," he would tell the boy who kept the carol

Staff 1908. Notable names include: Middle row, E. T. Schoedelin (far left), F. Cunningham Woods (4th left), Revd G. W. Douton (5th left). Front row, C. A. Evors (far left) and Revd A. E. Allcock (middle).

[imposition] book. That was the sort of thing that went on ... It wasn't just book-work that you learned at Highgate. I was a very happy boy there' (Kay).

There were other well-liked masters, particularly Evors. He was 'the most popular of all', Taylor remembered. 'He didn't spoil anybody, but he would listen to you.' None of the boys of Allcock's time whose reminiscences were collected in the 1980s mentioned a single master they disliked.

In other ways Highgate was exceptional for the time. Food for boarders was more than adequate. Breakfast at School House was a kind of lunch, served by a butler, including porridge and bacon, with beer instead of tea or coffee; the dormitories were divided into individual cubicles; and School House had its own sanatorium, run by Miss Crich. 'She was a wonderful nurse,' though her methods were traditional. 'I always associate that room with leeches' (Taylor).

In one way, however, the school failed to fulfil Allcock's hopes for it. In 1895 when the new buildings were first discussed by the Governors, it had 274 boys (223 seniors, fifty-one juniors). By 1906 it had 324. But in 1908, the year in which failing eyesight led to Allcock's resignation, it had contracted again to 295.

7

AN AEROPLANE ON THE ROOF – JOHNSTON ELEVATES SCIENCE 1908–1936

IN CHOOSING JOHN ALEXANDER Hope Johnston, a 37-year-old Scot, to succeed Allcock, the Governors abandoned a well-established nineteenth-century tradition: that a public school headmaster should be in holy orders. They were not the first to do so; five years earlier when Marlborough appointed Frank Fletcher *The Times* described him as 'one lay apple in the clerical dumpling'. Highgate had had clerics as its Head Masters for almost 200 years, since the resignation of Henry Mills in 1712. The new Head Master quickly overcame one consequent problem – that he had no right to preach in chapel – by becoming a lay reader.

Without doubt Johnston will be judged Highgate's most important Head Master of the twentieth century. Underlying everything he did for the school was his enthusiasm for mathematics and science. He himself had been Professor of Physics at the Royal Agricultural College, Cirencester, 14th wrangler at Cambridge, and for the last ten years a teacher of science and maths at Tonbridge School.

It was to other matters, however, that he first gave his attention, showing that his ambitions for Highgate were in many ways similar to those of his predecessors: to make it as respected a public school as the best in the country. Since these were predominantly boarding schools, he set about increasing the number of Highgate's boarders, persuading the Governors not only to prepare a new prospectus 'with photographs', but to allow him to place advertisements for the school in newspapers in Capetown, Johannesburg, Buenos Aires and Calcutta.

In one way he was quickly successful. Numbers rose from the 295 he had inherited to 480 in the autumn of 1913, then to 603 in May 1921. But the

John Alexander Hope Johnston, Head Master 1908–36: a contemporary caricature.

Highgate contingent at OTC Camp, Farnborough, 1909. At far right is C. A. Evors, staff 1885–1929.

proportion of boarders had only now risen to a quarter of the total (172), and it was only in the 1920s that he was able to open a succession of new boarding houses: Grindal (1920), Cordell (1921), Mansfield (1923), Field (1929), and for junior boys Bishop Sandys (1925); and it was only in May 1928 that boarders for the first time exceeded day boys in number (344 against 337). It was Johnston's bad luck that the Depression then halted expansion. By the autumn term of 1936 there were only a handful more (684), of whom only 246 were boarders and he had had to close Mansfield and Bishop Sandys.

Meanwhile, to encourage the sort of house loyalty and inter-house rivalry of a boarding school, he abandoned the old lettered houses for day boys and divided them into houses according to the areas in which their homes lay: Northgate, Eastgate, Westgate, Middlegate, Fargate and Southgate. The school also lacked a uniform, something other public schools had been steadily adopting for fifty years and Johnston tried to introduce one; old photographs, however, show much variety of dress, and boys of the time remembered that on weekdays a sober suit of some sort was all that was enforced for seniors. All wore red caps to come to school but blazers were only compulsory for juniors.

Johnston made another change. Until now parents who sent their boys to the Junior School were under no obligation to send them on to the Senior School. From 1916 he gave 'priority of admission' to boys whose parents intended to do so. Highgate, he considered, was now able to 'reap the rewards of its own previous labours'.

More important than any of these changes to the school's shape and organisation were those to its curriculum. Despite Allcock's support for modern

'Highgate School' from Throne and Country, *12 February 1910.*

subjects, Highgate had essentially remained a school where 'the classical side was what mattered, and the modern side was a concession to pressures from parents for some teaching other than Greek and Latin' (Kay). Johnston changed all this, within a few years starting a science side in parallel to the classical and modern sides.

From his arrival the boys found Johnston alarming. He went through the school 'like a tornado' (Freckerick Molz 1907–15). He would enter chapel in his gown, carrying his mortarboard, from a doorway beside the organ and come down the aisle to his seat like 'a ship in full sail ... He was an overpowering

F. Cunningham Woods, music master, 1896–1927, and the Orchestra, c. 1910

sight, no question of that ... Mrs Johnston was a charming woman. People used to wonder how a woman like that could marry such a horror.'

A famous sight of those days, Reginald Hosford (1910–15) remembered, was the Head Master marching up Hampstead Lane to school.

> There was this towering figure, for he was not only a very big man but a very tall man, and he had a very large overcoat on, and over the overcoat he used to wear his school gown. You had this terrific figure marching up with a crowd of boys, but completely separate from them – he never walked with a boy, or a boy with him – this great figure marching up Hampstead Lane. He went marching down again as well, of course, but you never seemed to see him then ... I'm sure he was enjoying every minute of it.

In 1913 there occurred one of those incidents, trivial in themselves, which become legend: the great hissing scandal. At the Christmas concert in Big School it was the custom for Old Cholmeleians and boys to prolong the final 's' of the word 'resonemus' in the song 'Dulce Domum'. When, to prevent this, Johnston ordered a new song, Douton, senior classics master, somewhat ineptly wrote one with a line which ended 'fundatoris'. The consequence could have been foreseen: 'It was a very successful hissing.' Molz remembered seeing Johnston stand up and glare at the back rows, his face livid. All who had hissed were told to report to him and perhaps fifty did (over 100 according to some boys), thinking there was safety in numbers. But Johnston caned every one of them. 'When the first

Football First XI, 1911 – three died in the First World War.

wretched people went in there, they got three each; there was a rush to be last – we thought he'd be weakening. But then somebody got four, and there was a rush for the doors.'

For Highgate, as for all British public schools, the First World War was the most traumatic of all its experiences. War was not unexpected, and in the previous ten years the Corps had become an increasingly important feature of the school's life. In 1908, as part of Haldane's army reforms, it had been renamed the Officers' Training Corps and transferred to the 7th Battalion of the Middlesex Regiment. At the same time one of its main features, the Certificate A examination, was made a more realistic preparation for a commission in the Territorial or regular Army. By 1914 half the officers of the 7th Middlesex had belonged to Highgate's Corps.

Sixty-five members went to the memorable Aldershot camp of July 1914. By the Sunday afternoon of that week 'there were all manner of rumours in the air and an uncanny feeling that a general mobilization might be ordered at any moment'. The news of this came the same night and at 7.30 next morning the school's unit, tents struck, marched out of camp. War was declared next day.

The November 1914 issue of *The Cholmeleian* republished a recruiting poem:

'We shall not need Conscription if you are keen enough to see,
That every boy at Highgate School should join the O.T.C.'

Seventy-five new recruits had already done so, bringing its strength to 150. A

Second Lieutenant Alexander Williamson, Seaforth Highlanders, an Old Cholmeleian on the school staff, became the first public school master to be killed in action in World War I.

Old Cholmeleian Society Dinner, 1913.

list followed of almost 300 Old Cholmeleians who were in the armed services. A few pages later came the first report of a school casualty: Second Lieutenant Alexander Williamson. Williamson had joined Highgate's Corps as a drummer in 1903 and risen to become Colour Sergeant. From Cambridge he had gone to Blundell's then returned in 1912 to teach at Highgate. 'We used to see this name in the school records', Hosford remembered, 'for the 100 yards, 10 seconds flat ... And then we were told that Williamson had been appointed to the staff, and we thought that now we were going to see this wonderful man, and he was almost venerated as a god; and he turned out to be an awfully nice chap. He started the school band in the OTC.' The day after war was declared Williamson reported for duty; two months later he was killed at the Battle of the Aisne.

By December the number of serving Old Cholmeleians had risen to 393, and the roll of dead to six. Meanwhile the Corps gained more recruits and by the summer of 1915 numbered 231. On 31 May that year, at 11.30 p.m., the first Zeppelin raider dropped bombs on Dalston. When another Zeppelin passed over the school that year, Molz, in the Sixth Form, remembered everyone rushing to the window to see it, including Johnston, who remarked, 'We live in stirring times, my masters.' Three years later (1918) 'The whole school was taken into the school field and made to lie flat on the grass while we watched the German planes flying over London. Later we picked up shrapnel from the field' (Anthony Plowman 1918–23).

The school was affected in other ways. By the time Ronald Macbeth (1917–22) arrived, life at School House was 'like being in prison'. For breakfast there was bread and scrape (margarine or dripping) with only occasionally a little

Procession from chapel after 350th Anniversary Service, 1915. Johnston immediately behind the last clergyman.

bit of bacon or an egg. For lunch there was often lentil pie. 'It was really rather galling to eat this stuff and see the headmaster necking into roast chicken ... it was always said that he had a gastric ulcer and that therefore he had to have a special diet. Most of us believed that as much as we believed any other fairy story.'

Meanwhile in July 1916 the first Battle of the Somme had been fought, at which the slaughter of the sort of young men whom the public schools of Britain produced (the officers of Kitchener's volunteer New Army) reached a climax. In all 221 Highgate boys died in the First World War. They are commemorated by the memorial which stands outside the chapel, designed by the Old Cholmeleian, Sir Reginald Blomfield.

It was in Johnston's report to the Governors on the year 1913 that he told them of a development of the school curriculum in which Highgate was leading the way. A master had been appointed to teach a new form on the modern side, the work of this form to be 'largely of a commercial character, particular attention being paid to Modern Languages, to Commercial Arithmetic, to Industrial History, and similar semi-technical subjects. This new feature of the school work', Johnston continued, 'appears to be enjoying the expected measure of success ... Indications exist that other Public Schools are about to follow in our footsteps.'

Science was at this time being taught in a ramshackle building to the north of Central Hall which included biology, physics and chemistry laboratories of a

Johnston and staff, c. 1920.

primitive sort and an art room. Its upper floor was connected to the gallery of Central Hall by an iron bridge. In the same report Johnston told the Governors that 'an extending and remodelling of the Science Building is in my opinion essential'. Despite the outbreak of war, he continued, year after year, to say similar things. 'I would beg you again to consider the urgent needs ... for wider and more modern Science accommodation' (January 1915). 'The problem of adequate laboratory accommodation becomes more acute every year (January 1916). 'The upper limit has almost been reached, and the walls of the laboratories

The unveiling of the 1914–18 War Memorial, 1921.

Start of the 1922 cross-country race in North Road.

refuse to expand' (January 1917). 'The demand for Science teaching is growing greater every day. I have enlarged on this question in every one of my Annual Reports for six years' (January 1918).

> The School at the present moment is on the wave of a high tide, which should be taken 'at the flood', but if one important step is postponed its fortunes, in my opinion, will slowly ebb away. New Science Buildings would not merely be an advantage; they have become a sheer necessity ... I think it well to inform you that wide and growing dissatisfaction with our present Science Buildings exists among the parents whose boys are now at the School ... The worst feature of all is that the best type of parent – the man of education and discrimination – frequently pays us a visit on the strength of our reputation and almost as frequently, after seeing our Science Buildings, shakes his head and departs (January 1919).

The conversion in 1921 of the Drill Hall in Castle Yard into 'a new and more commodious workshop' freed the old workshop to be transformed into the school's best science laboratory, but Johnston was far from satisfied. 'At the risk of wearisome repetition, I cannot urge too strongly the increasing necessity for new and extensive Science Buildings' (April 1922). Only in 1925 was he at last able to say, 'It is with feelings of very profound relief that I view the advent of the new Science Building, so long needed and desired.'

On 21 July 1928 came the great day, described by Johnston as 'The most notable public occasion in our history', when the new Science Building was formally opened by the Minister for Air, Sir Samuel Hoare. 'The new

Above: *Highgate boys at Bisley, 1921.*

Above right: *Dr Johnston and Sir Samuel Hoare, Minister for Air, opening the New Science Block, 1928.*

quadrangle', Johnston subsequently told the Governors, 'was packed with an audience composed of many distinguished visitors, the Governors, Masters, parents and Old Boys of the School.' In the new laboratories boys were at work, and 'for the first time in their lives in probably the great majority of cases, grown-up people were able to see for themselves what is meant by practical work in every department of Science ... Over 600 people had lunch in marquees over the School Fields.' At the opening Johnston declared, 'This is no mere traditional home for physics and chemistry.' In the new building 'the budding engineer' would 'study the engines themselves, their principles of action, as well as their construction, and these are not merely the machines that rule the land and water, but, in response to a growing and natural demand, the engines and machines also which have achieved the conquest of the Air.'

When Sir Samuel Hoare toured the building he was particularly interested by the 'Snipe' aeroplane in the wood workshop. The Sopwith Snipe was the last rotary-engined fighter of the First World War. If Sir Samuel had climbed to the top of the new building he would have found a second aeroplane, an Avro 504K, housed in a hangar specially built for it at the cost of £639. He might also have found in the metal workshop five aeroplane engines. Most of this equipment had been given or loaned by the RAF. In charge of it, and of the School's Aeronautics Class was J. Wilkinson, a retired RAF sergeant major.

Geoffrey Buck (1935–40) remembered Wilkinson's classes. 'The good sergeant ... put my age-group fairly thoroughly through the hoop! We completely dismantled the "Avro" airframe at least on one side ... We also stripped and reassembled the "Monosoupape" Gnome engine of the 504K, the

Rolls-Royce "Eagle", the air-cooled Mercedes-Benz 6-cylinder reputed to be from a Fokker D7 and a small air-cooled radial engine, I think an Armstrong-Siddely "Lynx".' The metal wings of a Westland 'Wapiti', on the other hand, which hung on the walls of the wood workshop remained decorative because, the boys assumed, airframes had all been wooden in Wilkinson's time in the RAF, and 'the Wapiti bits and pieces were as much a closed book to him as they were to us'.

Highgate's Aeronautics Class was a concrete embodiment of Johnston's belief that education should fit boys for the world of their day; they should become 'air-minded'. It put Highgate ahead of any school in the country in the teaching of technology. This did not go unnoticed. In July 1930 the Prince of Wales (later Edward VIII, then Duke of Windsor) visited Highgate where he was shown engines 'in different stages of completion' in the metal workshop; a process of dyeing in the large lecture theatre; the Biological Laboratory, where he took 'considerable interest in the various forms of life found in the Empire', and a French class being taught by Linguaphone. In the Advanced Laboratory he was particularly interested by the preparation of a chemical used as dope for aeroplane fabric. In the hangar he 'talked for some minutes with Sgt.-Maj. Wilkinson, who, he discovered, had taken him for one of his earliest aeroplane flights'.

The same year the *Boys' Own Paper* published a feature on the Aeronautics Class which caused Lucien Wigdor (1933–6) to pester his father until he was sent to the school. Marcel Desoutter, a pre-First World War aviator, and Sir Alliot Verdon-Roe, founder of Avro, also sent their sons.

Sex education was another matter to which Johnston turned his active mind; if his views and proposals were those of the period, he was making them at a time when most schools were ignoring the question. In 1946 the starting of sex teaching at Marlborough provoked an attempted coup against the headmaster. Nineteen years earlier Johnston had written to parents,

> it has always been the rule for the House Master to see [boys] individually, in private, and to give them in discreet and well chosen words the kind of instruction which boys are otherwise apt to acquire in imperfect and unfortunate ways, sometimes from polluted sources and through impure

The revolutionary Aeronautics classrooms in the New Science Block, 1928

Above left: *Boys working on the Avro 504K, housed in its own specially built hangar.*

Above: *The Sopwith Snipe in the wood workshop.*

The Prince of Wales and Dr Johnston, July 1930.

'Dr Johnston and Sex', 1917. The leaflet warned parents of the need for a degree of sex education in times of war.

C. A. Evors, staff 1885–1929.

channels. The general state of public opinion and the distinct lowering in moral tone which accompanies a great war render it extremely necessary ... for House Tutors to extend this teaching and advice to Day Boys, after they are 13 years of age, together with a reverent treatment of the sex question and wise counsel on the Laws of Health and personal purity.

Memorable masters of Johnston's time included the mathematician, John Llewelyn Thomas (1915–47). 'Bookie' Thomas, so called because he ran the school's bookshop, claimed that he could multiply one sixteen-figure number by another sixteen-figure number in his head. 'It would take him two hours and give him an enormous headache, but he could do it ... He was such a gentle person in the classroom, probably too gentle ... he was very easily taken for a ride, and it was only if you really wanted to learn that you could learn enormously' (Jim Lindsay, 1928–34). Another maths master, Harold Sylvanus (1915–40), had come to Highgate when forced to close his own tutorial school in France after catching typhoid from Portuguese oysters. He taught a junior form until Johnston discovered his talent and promoted him to the Mathematics Sixth. Sylvanus's enthusiasms ranged from yachting and chess to the life of Napoleon and the sonnets of Shakespeare.

A well-remembered science master was Alfred Izard (1905–41). It was Izard who coached Hosford and two other boys for the first medical examination attempted from the school. 'He took it very seriously, and got us through, too. It was considered rather a triumph for the science staff.' But he was also 'a great comedian ... when he was taking one of the lower classes ... The sort of thing that he would do was to take up this rubber tubing and use it as a catapult, and if he saw a boy on the other side of the room fooling about, this chap would as likely as not find this piece of rubber tubing coming at him.'

Subjects which were expanded in these years included Spanish, though Highgate's Spanish teachers found the job a testing one. Between 1914 and 1925 no fewer than nine came and went. Languages were now mostly taught by the direct method, but the French teacher, Emile Thaddée Schoedelin (later Sheldon) (1894–1934) retained methods of earlier times, standing his class in a circle and asking questions along the line, promoting the first boy to answer correctly above those who had failed and awarding marks according to final positions. Charles Walford (1903–12), who taught the Third Form wearing a stiff white collar 3½ inches deep, seemed even more a relic, and was described by the boys as 'a donkey looking out of a whitewashed stall' (Molz).

Four masters besides Schoedelin who had been appointed in the previous century, survived through the war into the 1920s: Evors, eventually known as 'The Old Man'; the classicist, the Revd George Douton, author of that unfortunate school song, who would teach in his mortarboard: 'he had very shaggy eyebrows, and the tassel used to catch in them'; Franklyn Lushington (1885–1930): seventy years later Arthur Barfield (1910–17) still remembered how Lushington would teach the rhythms of hexameter and pentameter: '"Dum-dum-dum-dum-dum, dum-diddle-dum-diddle-dum" – we all had to recite this'; and the Revd Sandford Simons, temporary head in 1893, another maths teacher, who 'used to go about with one of those long wooden compasses' which he called his 'persuader'.

A master who arrived in the same year as Johnston but outlasted him was the famous soccer player, the Revd Kenneth Hunt (1908–45). Hunt had played for Wolverhampton Wanderers, and taken part in both the amateur and the professional Cup Finals, scoring in the latter in 1908. Like other clerics on the staff, Hunt never showed any intention of becoming a parish priest, indeed some boys considered that he did not have 'a very profound feeling for his vocation', and though he became school chaplain, he was also head of games and for four years commander of the OTC. Barfield remembered discussing with a friend how Hunt and his wife got along with each other and concluding, as Milton might have, 'he for football only, she for footballing him'.

Better known outside Highgate than any other master of Johnston's time was Thomas Stearns Eliot, who taught at the Junior School for three terms in 1916. Here at the Junior School he was overlapped by Highgate's best known boy of the time, John Betjeman. Betjeman was already writing poetry and remembered

Sketch of E. T. Sheldon (formerly Schoedelin), staff 1894–1934.

Revd G. W. Douton, staff 1885–1924, at his desk.

Staff football XI v. The School, 1913. The great K. R. G. Hunt (scorer for Wolverhampton Wanderers in the 1908 FA Cup Final) is third from the left, middle row.

showing Eliot a collection to which he had given the title *The Best Poems of Betjeman*, but what Eliot thought of them he never discovered and the manuscript is lost.

Betjeman disliked Highgate, remembering being bullied by his contemporaries and ill-treated by Edward Kelly, Master-in-Charge of the Junior School.

> ... how Kelly stood us in a ring:
> 'Three sevens, then add eight, and take away
> Twelve; what's the answer?' Hesitation then
> Meant shaking by the shoulders till we cried.

Betjeman certainly exaggerated the horrors of his later school, Marlborough, and may have done so of Highgate. Sir Anthony Plowman (1918–23) thought Kelly 'no Wackford Squeers ... and I was in his form for at least a year', and T. S. Eliot remembered him in his spare time making wooden splints for wounded soldiers. But Thomas Bayley, who arrived in 1910, had all too convincingly vivid memories of Kelly:

> The wrongness of the man was that he *set out* to reduce a small boy to tears by bullying and jeering, and couldn't stop until he had succeeded ... I have a clear picture in my mind of his form. Especially of one day when it was my turn to stand out and repeat the Latin sentences, with a flick of the stick after each word. 'The horse and the dog are friends to man' – Equus (swipe), et (swipe), canis (swipe). Allowable for one or two sentences, perhaps, but it would continue until the inevitable happened, and he grabbed the back of your Eton collar and started to shake you, still using the stick after each word ... The worst sufferer was my then friend, R. T. 'Brab' Heaton-Ellis ... I've seen Kelly shake 'Brab' until he had burst

his collar from the studs and then hurl him out of the room. If only the wretched man could have given us a few strokes and then forgotten it, I would have thought better of him. But he clearly enjoyed his bullying.

Bayley also remembered the Junior School's Play Room. 'On winter evenings we would be turned in there after tea. I can't remember any kind of game or book being available, and I think it was a completely bare empty place. No master ever came near us. Our only occupation was a kind of all-in wrestling or Touch – merely rushing about the room until bedtime.'

Though boys found Johnston as alarming as Kelly, they did not dislike, indeed many admired, him. They were amazed by his memory. 'He could tell at any time of day where any form should be and what they were supposed to be doing.' And Molz among others came to like him. Aged 17, when the First World War began, he wanted at once to join the Army, and his parents asked Johnston to give him advice. 'He made me sit down, and talked to me like a Dutch Uncle – he really was very kind. He said "Look, one thing I can tell you is that this war won't be over in six months – it'll go on for three years." I've never forgotten that.'

The staff, on the other hand, were never reconciled to Johnston. According to Hosford 'they absolutely hated him'. When Hosford became school doctor in 1934 he remembered 'Johnston sending for me and behaving as if I was still a boy, and having a most exhaustive and informed questioning from Johnston – he thought he knew about everything, including medical matters, so that he was almost telling me how to be a school doctor.' Hosford supported the general suspicion that Johnston was a heavy drinker. 'He came from Tonbridge School and he was known there, we heard later, as "The Boozer".' According to

A. H. Fabian and L. Aguirre – the greatest pair of a great fives tradition. Fabian was both an Old Cholmeleian and on the staff, and played for Derby County and the Corinthians. Aguirre was killed in the Spanish Civil War. Photograph c. 1930

The final of the 120 yards Open Hurdles, 1918.

Above: R. W. V. Robins, pupil 1921–5 and later England cricket captain, dressed as Charlie Chaplin, c. 1922.

Above right: Athletics team, 1921. The captain, Douglas Lowe (centre), went on to win two Olympic 800 metre gold medals in 1924 and 1928.

Hosford, when Geoffrey Bell, Johnston's successor, first came to dinner with Johnston, Bell could not understand why Johnston kept leaving the room, and only subsequently deduced that it was for additional 'liquid refreshment'.

More objectionable to the masters was their belief that he was exploiting the school for his own financial benefit. His remuneration, generally believed to be the largest of any headmaster in the country, included a capitation fee of nearly £5 a pupil, and this, they considered, induced him to expand the school beyond the numbers it could properly take. They also criticised the way in which he cut the school off from the village. 'When I was first appointed', Thomas Twidell (1922–62) remembered, 'the people of the village said that in the old days they could go on the school site and were welcomed, but now we're chivvied off.'

In Hosford's opinion, however, there was a more basic reason for their hostility. 'He treated them so badly. He didn't seem to have any kind or nice feelings for them at all. He regarded them as his enemies and there's no doubt that they regarded him as their enemy ... I got to know a number of the masters very well in those days, and there was hardly a soul who ever said anything good about him.'

In the 1920s the staff still had no pension scheme and, as the historian N. B. C. Lucas would tell the story, considered there was no chance of obtaining Johnston's support for one. They therefore decided to approach the Governors directly, but, realising that Johnston would dismiss whoever did so, drew lots. The lot fell to Lucas, he approached the Governors and obtained their agreement to a scheme, but he was duly dismissed by Johnston (Lucas became headmaster of Midhurst Grammar School).

AN AEROPLANE ON THE ROOF — JOHNSTON ELEVATES SCIENCE

Fortunately for Highgate, Johnston's personal ambition led to an overwhelming amibition for the school. Success of any sort contributed to the fulfilment of this and he was as keen about the school's athletics as he was about its work. In 1922 he acquired Far Field to provide the extra sports ground by then badly needed. On the Junior Field he had built a new group of fives courts, so enabling Highgate to remain the country's leading Eton fives school, with more courts than Eton itself.

He was lucky in the 1920s to have a number of outstanding games players and athletes in the school, some of whom became world famous. Best known of these was the cricketer, R. W. V. Robins (1921–5) who later played for England against South Africa, New Zealand, India and the West Indies, and who captained the MCC in the 1936–7 series against Australia. A full-page cartoon in *The Cricketer* of 5 August 1922, celebrating Highgate's famous defeat of Essex, showed Robins performing with bat and ball, and commented 'R. W. V. Robins (age 16) made 52 in style. Whether batting or bowling, he had all the assurance of an old Pro.' It also showed 'the Head and the Head's Good Lady' watching, Johnston in a trilby, with magnificent looped moustache and satisfied grin.

Well known as a runner was Douglas Lowe (1917–21). Lowe was captain of cricket and football, and played for the school at fives, but it was at the half-mile that he excelled, winning the event at the public school sports in 1920. In 1924 he won the Olympic gold medal at the 800 metres in Paris (at the Olympics made famous by the film, *Chariots of Fire*). From 1939 to 1975 he was a school Governor, acting as Treasurer and Chairman for the last ten years.

Johnston's satisfaction at such successes showed in his reports to the Governors. In 1929 he told them

> The Fives Six has again gone through the season without losing a match and achieved the astonishing result of beating Cambridge University ... represented by an exceptionally strong pair of Old Harrovians, who ... subsequently declared that the School's First pair was the finest pair of

Detail from The Cricketer, *August 1922; Johnston, Mrs Johnston and Albert Knight, ex-Leicestershire and England, the school's cricket professional.*

Cricket on the Senior Field in the 1920s.

Football coaching by Maurice Edelston of Fulham FC (far right), c. 1934–5. A. H. Fabian second from right.

school boys they had ever played ... Continuing his brilliant career at Cambridge, R. W. V. Robins ... reached the summit of his fame in the Lord's match *versus* Oxford in July, for in addition to capturing eight Oxford wickets ... he scored innings of 53 and 101 not out, thus joining the notable few who have scored a century in the Oxford and Cambridge match. At the Olympic Games at Amsterdam, D. G. A. Lowe was, for the second time in his life, the winner of the 800 metres race, and this he accomplished in record Olympic time. Running later on in Berlin during the German championships, he achieved the distinction of winning the same event in world record time.

Johnston also regularly reported the school's academic successes. In 1919 he told the Governors that it had gained six scholarships at the older universities and two important awards at the University of London. In 1928 he reported 'A record number of open Awards ... at the Universities of Oxford and Cambridge where members of the school have won three scholarships for Classics, one Scholarship and one Exhibition for Natural Sciences, one Scholarship for Mathematics ... and an Exhibition for Modern Languages, a total of seven in all ... at least one award for Modern Languages has been gained during every one of the last six years.'

Even Hosford, who as the school's doctor probably heard more criticism of Johnston than anyone else, considered him 'a very extraordinary character', who 'made the school what it is today'.

8

ANOTHER WAR
1936–1954

'AH, NOW WE'VE GOT A GENTLEMAN,' one member of Common Room is said to have remarked when he heard of the appointment of Johnston's successor. There was no doubt about that. Geoffrey Foxall Bell had been head boy of Repton (under two future archbishops, William Temple and Geoffrey Fisher), then a cricket blue at Balliol, where he read history. In the war he had served in the Royal Field Artillery, and been awarded the MC. He was also a schoolmaster with wide experience, having taught in Canada (his wife was half Canadian), at Christ's Hospital, and for the last nine years at Trent College, Derbyshire, where he was headmaster. But it was the title of the book he published nine years after he retired which better suggests his special contribution to Highgate: *Establishing a Fruit Garden* (1963).

Characteristic of Bell's belief that Highgate should provide opportunities for boys who were not academically outstanding nor successful at traditional team games (and of his admiration for Kurt Hahn, the German Jewish refugee founder of Gordonstoun) was his creation of the Pioneers, a group of boys who, among other things, built a school tennis court and a Junior School playground. He also founded a troop of scouts at the school and elevated tennis to a school game. He encouraged a great spawning of societies, five of which were founded in his first year: the Photographic Society, the Political Club, the Modern Language Circle, the Modelling Club and the Leonardo Society (to sponsor museum visits). And in the summer of 1939 there appeared an independent school magazine, *The Forum*.

There had been previous independent school and house magazines. In 1896 *A Resurrection Pie* began its first issue with a parody *Ingoldsby Legend* entitled 'Speech Day':

> The Head sits square in the library chair
> And looks at the guests assembled there;

Geoffrey Foxall Bell, Head Master 1936–54.

OTC Inspection Day, 1937, Senior Field.

> Ladies and gentlemen, girls and boys
> (The latter producing considerable noise),
> Masters sedate, and governors great,
> All seated around the angelical Pate,
> Who calmly sits thinking, and winking, and blinking,
> As jabbering on at a terrible rate,
> The great G**rge L**ch is making his speech:
> Three yards is as far as his voice will reach,
> And a chap at the door most solemnly swore
> He heard the angelic Head Master snore!

In 1924, Philip Harben, future TV chef, edited several issues of *The Porto*. It was 'always ready to expose abuses', its first editorial announced, adding 'Evidence must be strictly attested'. *The Forum*, largest yet in format, aimed more ambitiously to be 'a record of the ideas of our contemporaries' which its readers would themselves provide. An article in the first issue on the Labour Party, by the history master, Thomas Fox (1934–73) examined a question which seems curiously perennial: 'When, some time this year, Mr Chamberlain deems the moment ripe for a dissolution of Parliament, Great Britain will have experienced fourteen years of Conservative government out of the last seventeen ... In British politics such a phenomenon demands some very special explanation.'

During his first three years – years overhung by the expectation of war – Bell moved the Junior School from Dyne's old house in Southwood Lane, where it had been since its foundation in 1889, to a newly built Cholmeley House in Bishopswood Road, modernised the three Dungeon classrooms below Big School where the three lowest forms were still taught, created the Jeudwine Library, named after the Governor, Edward Jeudwine, who made the major contribution to it, and with the help of an appeal which raised £982, started work on an open-air swimming pool on the slope below today's Dyne House.

At the same time Bell considered with increasing urgency what the school should do if war came. In April 1938 he and his family made a reconnaissance, staying at the North Devon resort of Westward Ho! And early in May, a week before the first Czechoslovakian crisis, he asked the Governors to consider air-raid precautions. But that September, when the second Czechoslovakian crisis occurred, he still had no firm instructions.

As a result, after Chamberlain's meetings with Hitler on 15 and 22 September had failed to produce any promise of peace, he sent two masters, Donald Gough (1925–60) and H. C. Wallwork (1928–47) to the West Country to reserve accommodation at hotels, boarding-houses or holiday camps. And on 28 September, when Chamberlain and Hitler were due to meet for the third time, he ordered evacuation. The Junior School went to Totnes, the boarders of Grindal to Ilfracombe and the remaining Senior School boarders to Westward Ho! The day boys were to have gone next, to an empty house near Horsham which a parent had offered, but before this could happen Chamberlain had returned from Munich waving his piece of paper and announcing 'Peace in our time'.

Whether or not Bell believed him, he realised that the evacuation had been premature, and next Monday, 3 October, the boys came back. All this had happened when many London schools had not even made plans for evacuation. The City of London School, for example, sited far more dangerously on the Embankment, was still negotiating its evacuation to Marlborough the following spring.

During 1939 Bell and the Governors considered three wartime alternatives: to stay at Highgate (but this might be impossible if the government requisitioned the school's buildings); to amalgamate with another school in the country (but this could lead to the school losing its individuality); or to repeat the evacuation, this time to a single safe place. They chose a modified form of the third alternative. The school would remain open at Highgate for boys whose parents wanted them to stay there. The rest would go to North Devon, the seniors to Westward Ho!, the juniors to Hartland Abbey.

In August 1939 Highgate again took early action. On the 24th an advance party left for Devon, and a notice was published in the press advising parents that the school would open there on the 28th. From the 26th boys began to arrive, by train, coach, car and bicycle, until, on Sunday 3 September when Chamberlain announced that we were at war, 356 seniors had assembled at Westward Ho! and 109 juniors at Hartland Abbey.

Westward Ho! had been created at the south-east corner of Bideford Bay in 1863 by Captain Molesworth of the Northam Burrows Hotel and Villa Company, with the idea that it would become a resort to rival Ilfracombe. It was named after Charles Kingsley's fictional celebration of the destruction of the Armada by the seamen of Devon. But the settlement had not been a success; the fashionable visitors Molesworth expected never came and its 600 foot pier was washed away by a storm before it had been completed. By 1939 it was a shabby

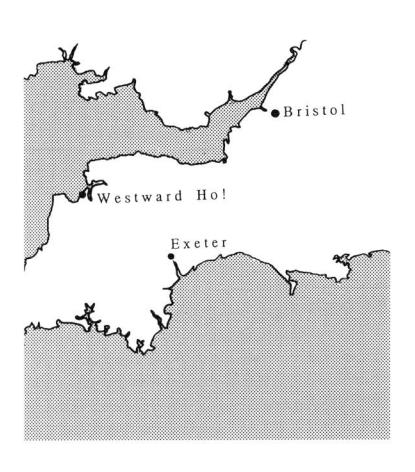

Illustrated Sporting & Dramatic News, *1939. Feature on Highgate at Westwood Ho!, Theodore Mallinson (staff 1939–72) taking PT on the beach.*

sprawl along a couple of miles of coast, with, as its only notable features, Torridge House – the bleak four-storey building which had once been the Imperial Service College – where Kipling set *Stalky & Co.* – and the Royal North Devon golf course.

Neither Torridge House, nor any of Westward Ho!'s hotels or boarding-houses had enough space for the whole school, and though it leased one other big house, Buckleigh Place, the Senior School needed to occupy more than a dozen Westward Ho! buildings. The difficulties this created can be imagined. It was a mile between the farthest apart of those near the beach, and about a mile inland to the Head Master's house, Bellevue. Furthermore the ground behind the beach rose sharply and many of the inland buildings could only be reached by a steep climb.

Though most classes were taken in rooms in the buildings where the boys slept, for a time three had to be taught at the Sunshine Café, in a single room divided by far from sound-proof partitions. And none of the houses provided any room which could be used as a laboratory; to remedy this Bell called down from London the science master Philip Bateman (1931–62) who transformed Twose's garage and stables into chemistry and physics laboratories.

To make it possible for boys to arrive at distant classrooms in time for lessons, breaks (and the lessons themselves) were lengthened. The weather could not be avoided so easily. When one class arrived soaked to the skin they had to be stripped naked while their clothes were dried. In January 1940, when Governor Jeudwine came to inspect the school, snow fell so heavily that he could not complete his tour. A few weeks earlier the photographer of the *Illustrated Sporting*

Lessons in the Sunshine Café: 'Jumbo' White's class.

& Dramatic News had been more successful and on 22 December 1939 the magazine published a four-page feature on Highgate at Westward Ho!

It showed the boys of the school at work and play, no longer wearing suits and caps but in blazers, open-neck shirt and shorts, the tender knees of Londoners exposed to Atlantic gales. Most memorably, it pictured the whole school at before breakfast PT doing knees-bend on the beach. 'Bell very often came round the squads', Theodore Mallinson (1939–72) remembered. 'He was a very active headmaster and encouraged us in that way.' Mallinson (whose call-up was deferred so that the school could retain at lest one young and able-bodied master) was made responsible for other hearty innovations: cross-country running, and night-long expeditions on the moors. One pair of boys 'saw the sun set on Dartmoor and rise on Exmoor, bicycling throughout the night'. Making an expedition of this sort was one of the qualifications for the County Badge, 'a kind of physical School Certificate', which also required a boy to achieve reasonable standards at running, athletics, throwing, jumping, swimming and first aid. The County Badge was later merged with the Duke of Edinburgh Award Scheme which the school joined in 1963. Boys who took a more academic interest in their new surroundings founded the Highgate Archaeological Society.

Traditional team games were much reduced, since Westward Ho!'s recreation-ground only had space for a single football pitch, or for a cricket pitch so fierce that one boy, hit on the chin by a ball, partially bit off the end of his tongue. As substitutes, golf and (until the beach was mined) sea-bathing or hockey on the sands were introduced.

Mallinson takes cross-country at Westward Ho!

With so many young masters absent, teaching at the school was not likely to be of pre-war standard, but boys continued to win Oxford and Cambridge scholarships, and two history masters were exceptional: Tommy Fox and Arthur Preston White (1919–51). Tom Sargant (1917–24) remembered how White 'had a most dramatic sense; he would act out the scenes. You had to listen to Preston White. I got a history prize ... entirely due to Preston White.' Twidell remembered White's 'ponderous style, which I suppose resulted in his being called Jumbo'. (White's 1914–18 letters home from the Western Front, *No Easy Hopes or Lies*, were published in 1991.)

Martin Gilbert, Churchill's biographer, who was taught by Fox after the war, compared him with another post-war history master, Alan Palmer.

> Tommy Fox ... was mocked by some boys as an eccentric. But his main 'eccentricity' was a great virtue, to refuse to accept the glib platitudes of the day ... and try to get boys to think for themselves. I once wrote a 'defence of democracy' essay for him, which led to a great debate! ... Without Tommy's willingness to enter into debates on these issues, to read what one had written, and to give encouragement, I doubt if I would have persevered.

ANOTHER WAR

> Alan Palmer ... taught the importance of narrative and chronology in history ... Under Alan, dates, individuals and places became facsinating points of reference rather than obstacles.
>
> Both Tommy Fox and Alan Palmer had the gift of making a young man ... feel ... that history, far from being engraved on rock tablets, was a fluid and fast-moving stream into which even a fifth-former could plunge and survive.

At Westward Ho! most boys belonged to the Corps, soon renamed the Junior Training Corps and dressed no longer in tunics with brass buttons but in battledress. Masters and older boys also joined the Home Guard, and others took part in typical wartime activities, raising loans for armaments at War Weapon Weeks and digging for victory. If sometimes the war seemed far away, German planes could often be heard passing overhead at night on their way to raid the towns of Wales and the West Midlands, occasionally a dog or a rabbit would detonate a land-mine on the beach, and at 5.00 one morning the school was woken by the enormous explosion of a sea-mine which had drifted ashore, Most of the windows in the High Street were shattered and its centre was piled with broken glass.

It was Hubert Gibbon (1922–65), Housemaster of the Lodge, who kept in touch with real war, writing continually to the many old boys who were in the services – by December 1940 he had sent them 700 letters. He also wrote the obituaries which *The Cholmeleian* soon began to publish. In total 176 Old Cholmeleians died serving in the Second World War. Gibbon, his wife and three other masters were officially thanked by the Governors for what they had done for the school at Westward Ho!, together with Mr Cartwright, head porter,

A. P. White (staff 1919–51) in 1950 with the Inspecting Officer. His First World War letters were published in 1991.

Westward Ho! OTC inspection.

105

later a Portsmouth publican, and Miss Bannister, the school secretary (1930–63). But the success of the venture was a joint achievement in which many others, boys as well as masters, played important parts.

While the Senior School suffered at Westward Ho! the senior boys of the Junior School enjoyed the comparative luxury of Hartland Abbey, fourteen miles to the west. Hartland had ceased to be an abbey in Henry VIII's reign, when it was demolished and given to the Sergeant of his cellar. In the second half of the eighteenth century it was rebuilt by the Sergeant's descendants in early Gothic Revival style, then in about 1860 'much was done to replace the happy gimcrack of a hundred years before by something sounder, thicker and more solid-looking' (Pevsner). Throughout these changes the old abbey's cloisters survived below ground level, and nothing could change the house's delightful setting, in a meadow, part way down the steep side of a Devon combe.

Here, for two years Onfrey William Dumaresq (1911–49) and his boys became virtually an independent school. They ate and were taught in the cloisters, slept on the ground and first floors, walked two miles to Hartland parish church on Sundays in crocodile, threw paper darts at the portraits of the owner's ancestors in the grandest of the ground floor rooms and published their own magazine, *The Abbey News*, duplicated by Joan Bannister, price 1*d*. This recorded such natural phenomena as the discovery of a heron with a leg frozen into the ice of the stream at the bottom of the combe. It was, indeed, the abbey's fine rural setting which made it such an educational experience for the London boys who went there. Early in 1940 the remainder of the Junior School joined them, living at a rest house near the abbey, and all stayed at Hartland until 1942, when there was space for them to be reunited with the Senior School at Westward Ho!

Meanwhile at Highgate, Twidell also ran a virtually independent school for boys whose parents had not wished them to go to Devon. It had been Twidell's suggestion, during the 1938 crisis, that the school should stay open at its Highgate premises, but he and his boys were continually forced to move from building to building as different ones were requisitioned by the National Provincial Bank or the Navy. At first the eighty-three seniors used Field House, while the twenty-one juniors used Ingleholme. From here the boarders (there were never less than ten and they were probably the only school boarders who stayed in London throughout the Blitz) went at night to sleep in the air-raid shelter at the main school. Day boys, on the other hand, were allowed during actual air raids each to decide whether or not to stay or go home; most went home and none was hurt.

During the War Twidell made a memorable attempt to stimulate his boys' intellectual life by inviting to his drawing room at Field House, to talk to the Sixth Form, two remarkable and contrasted lecturers: Arthur Waugh, publisher and scholar, father of Alec and Evelyn Waugh; and Albert Knight, self-educated cricketer who had played for England and was the school's cricket professional.

> Mr Waugh [Alfred Doulton wrote, in his history of these years] was a Victorian by upbringing, silver-haired and venerable, who preferred to stand with his back to the fireplace; Mr Knight sat cross-legged in a

comfortable chair, displaying between the bottom of his trousers and the tops of his thick grey socks an expanse of white, woollen under-pants ... Mr Waugh spoke excitingly of the Victorian poets and the Pre-Raphaelites as though they were all his friends whom he had just left and he had come to tell us about them, Mr Knight discoursed ... on 'the History of Philosophy', beginning with the early Greek philosophers and ending ... with Einstein.

By May 1940 Field House had become too small for the senior boys, now increased to 122, and they moved to Johnston's Science Building. They were there that September, during the heaviest raids (when an average of 200 bombers attacked London every night) and spent much time in its basement shelter. A year later (September 1941) the Admiralty requisitioned the main school buildings, naming them HMS *President IV*, and the boys had to move across Southwood Lane to the old Cholmeley House, Dyne's one-time residence.

Finding staff was as much a problem for Twidell at Highgate as it was for Bell in Devon and he had to make unusual appointments: W. D. Deutsch, for example, a Hungarian from Vienna. When one maths master, S. P. Dienes, abruptly abandoned Highgate for Dartington Hall, no one remained who could coach a particular boy, Philip Escreet, for his mathematical scholarship exam. Eventually Gabbitas, Thring & Co offered an Indian, Mr Kali. This, Twidell remembered, set him a problem – Highgate had never before appointed a coloured master – and he consulted Sir Roger Hetherington, Chairman of the Governors.

> Hetherington: 'Is he black?'
> Twidell: 'Yes, sir.'
> Hetherington: 'Is he fat or slim?'
> Twidell: 'Slim, sir.'
> Hetherington: 'All right, appoint him.'

Kali proved an excellent teacher of mathematics and Escreet obtained his Christ Church scholarship.

Twidell's wife (he married in December 1940) was a particular help to him, acting as the school's caterer and matron, but with far wider supporting roles. It was Twidell himself, however, who should be given the main credit for the success of Highgate's wartime rump. He not only undertook the whole administration of his school with no secretary, but taught full time. Afterwards he claimed that all the normal subjects were taught throughout the school and the usual certificate examinations taken.

In essence the evacuation to Devon transformed a day school into a boarding school. For boys and masters this was in many ways a rewarding change, which in the end did no harm to the school, and it became a mainly day school again without difficulty when it returned to London. The evacuation did, however, do serious temporary damage. 'To take a North London school to the Devonshire coast', Twidell later said, 'seems to me to be the craziest thing you can possibly do; separating the boys far, far away from their parents, to start off with; secondly you get no new boys at all.' The evacuated school indeed shrunk from its original 465 to a mere

Cartoons by Gerard Hoffnung.

Above: *Self-portrait.*

Below: *Caricature of a Master, drawn by Hoffnung when he was a pupil at Highgate.*

Facing page: *A Highgate schoolboy.*

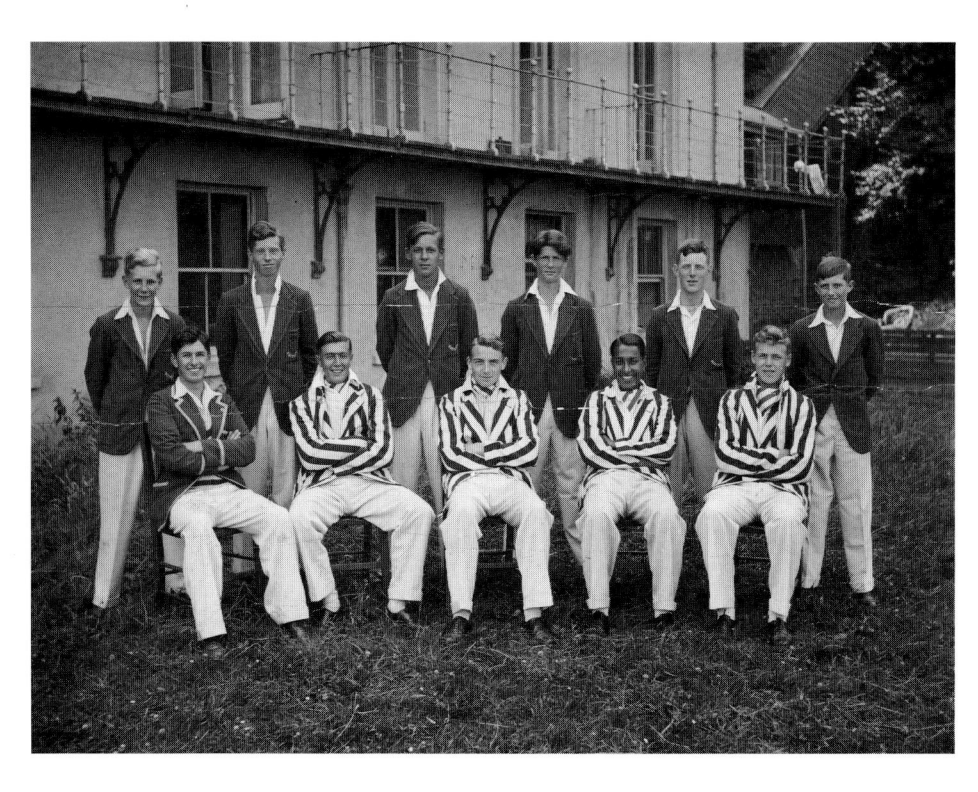

Cricket XI, Westward Ho!, 1941.

226, and a gain at Highgate (where there were 191 boys by January 1943) did not compensate for such a loss.

As a result the school experienced a financial crisis. It had never been well endowed, but depended on its pupils' fees, so such a fall in numbers was serious. Furthermore, in 1939 it had outstanding mortgages of £17,500 and £25,000, the second raised to finance the building of the new Cholmeley House for the Junior School. As the problem became more worrying, an economy discussed by the Governors was reducing the salaries of staff by suspending contributions to their pension fund. Though this was not done, Bell and the highest paid assistant master, Bateman, took voluntary reductions of £250 and £100 a year respectively. Despite economies, it seemed clear to Bell by September 1942 that the evacuation was proving a financial disaster, and he persuaded the Governors to write to parents asking whether they would prefer a return to Highgate the following January or in May. January became impossible when the Admiralty threatened to requisition School House and Grindal (in addition to the main school buildings), so eventually it was on 31 March that twenty-one railway containers and three furniture vans brought the school's possessions back from Westward Ho!, to be ready for a reopening of the whole school at Highgate for the summer term of 1943.

Considered in isolation, the school's evacuation may seem to have been a mistake, but schools which stayed in London also suffered sharp declines in numbers. At University College School these fell by about 50 per cent, and at King's College School, Wimbledon, from 585 to 435 (though admittedly by the autumn of 1942 they had recovered to 554). Some of the schools which were

108

ANOTHER WAR

evacuated suffered even more severely than Highgate; Mill Hill which went to St Bees in Cumberland, lost 42 per cent, falling from 344 to under 200, the City of London School which went to Marlborough fell from 741 to 499, and Westminster, which came and went to three different places, from 339 to 146. The wisest thing which Highgate did was to return to its catchment area ahead of other evacuated schools.

Much had changed at Highgate, where the staff now began to prepare for the summer term. Sidney Kipping (1921–45) described his first morning in his study at his old house, Cordell. Having dragged in a table and chair he felt he was 'getting on pretty well, but the sentiment was quite premature. A man called to "disconnect the electricity". I pointed out that I was engaged in moving *in*, not out, but he said it was necessary to disconnect it after the last lot went out. When the argument was over and he had gone, I persuaded myself that I should now be able to settle to letters. This was the signal for a GPO man to come and say he must "disconnect the telephone" – which he did. As I couldn't think of anything else that anybody could disconnect except the gas and water, I returned to my table and chair and the letter. At this juncture, however, an area of the ceiling left its accustomed place.'

A month later when the school reopened many inconveniences remained. Since the Navy still occupied the main school buildings, it was the boarding houses and Dyne House which had to provide classrooms and laboratories as well as boarding accommodation, and the chapel which had to be used for the first assembly. But already there was a small rise in numbers, from 417 which the two parts of the school had totalled in January to 430. Next term there was a further fifty and at the end of that year the Navy finally handed back the main school buildings.

The playing-fields were also much changed. The Senior Field was in fair condition, but Far Field was still partly an RAF lorry park, and on Junior Field vegetables grew among the wrecked sheds and concrete debris left by 906 Balloon Barrage Squadron. Everywhere grass was of meadow length.

Below left: *Damage to the roof of School House after a V-1 'Doodle Bug' landed on the Senior Field, 28 June, 1944.*
Below: *The crater.*

Caricature of E. F. Bullin, staff 1913–46.

The school's early return seemed badly timed the following summer (1944), when the V-1 attacks on London began. Mallinson remembered his colleague, Hunt, telling him that a V-1 would never get up Highgate Hill. He was wrong. At midday on 28 June one landed on Senior Field, between its second cricket-pitch and pavilion (the old gym). Fortunately the boys were at work, but one class was in the pavilion, being taken by Edward Bullin, an elderly bald master known as 'the Egg'.

According to Kyffin Williams (art master 1944–73) Bullin 'acted as a magnet to these bombs. Blown out of his house in Talbot Road, he moved to Bisham Gardens, only to be blasted from there. Finally, while he was taking a class in the cricket pavilion, one landed on the pitch outside. There was a terrible bang and the interior of the pavilion became a haze of dust and plaster. When this had subsided there was no sign of the Egg, and a blackboard lay over his desk. Eventually, composed and undefeated, Edward Bullin emerged, yet again unscathed.' Mrs Bell also had an escape. Normally at that time of day she sat at a particular window, practising the cello, but she happened to be away. The window was shattered and the pictures across the room were pierced with jagged daggers of glass. In fact no one was injured, but the roofs of the Senior as well as the second pavilion were badly damaged, and the danger of further bombs seemed serious enough for the school to plan not to reassemble in September but to teach by post. This proved unnecessary because by then the Germans had lost the French coast.

In 1945 the school, now fully re-established in its pre-war premises, seemed superficially to be the school it had been in the summer of 1939. Below the surface, however, there had been significant changes. Gibbon put first among

Dedication of the Memorial Gates, 1947: the procession from St Michael's church.

110

Above: *Dedication of the Memorial Gates, 1947.*

Above left: *Dedication of the Shakespeare Steps, 1947.*

these a decline in the power of prefects and the development of a more democratic atmosphere. This was given concrete form with the establishment in 1948 of a Consultative Assembly, where boys could debate the affairs of the school. A more tangible change was the continuing decline in the numbers of boarders. Before the war this had already seemed a problem to Housemasters, who, as at other schools, lived on the profits of their houses, but the Governors had taken no action. In January 1943 they decided to buy out the Housemasters.

During the following years Bell resumed his pre-war policy of broadening the activities of the school so that it would give more boys a beneficial and enjoyable time. Old societies were revived and new ones established. One of these, the Masaryk Society, he started in order to give senior boys the chance to hear 'well-informed public men and women talking on subjects of world-wide significance'. First to come was Jan Masaryk, at the time deputy prime minister of Czechoslovakia. Masaryk, according to *The Cholmeleian*, said little about his father, Thomas, first President of Czechoslovakia, after whom the society was named, but 'spent most of his time on a fascinating series of personal reminiscences'. On 20 November 1961 the Society heard a less well-known speaker, Mrs Margaret Thatcher, from the Ministry of Pensions and National Insurance, who spoke on Health Service problems and 'answered questions competently ... This was an important occasion as it was the first time the Society had been addressed by a member of the government in office.'

Societies and activities started in Devon now came to London. The Archaeological Society, which admitted that it had become 'rather moribund' because it had explored all the sites near Westward Ho!, was revitalised. On its first outing it found St Bartholomew-the-Great 'rigidly locked against us', but visited St Sepulchre's near by, the largest City church. Expeditions, of the sort previously made to Dartmoor and Exmoor, were now made from Highgate. Typically, on 20 May 1944, eighteen boys set out for the woods of Gomshall, near Dorking, to look for the memorial to Soapy Sam, Bishop Wilberforce. Fourteen were successful and slept the night in haystacks or barns.

Above: *Self-caricature of Kyffin Williams, RA, Head of Art 1944–73.*

Above right: *Some participants in the Second Junior School pageant, 1953.*

The school's Dramatic Society had been founded in 1934, as a result of the enthusiasm of the master, John Stephenson (1924–62), and had staged its first play, *She Stoops to Conquer*, the following year. Two plays a year were then performed at Highgate, and while in Devon no fewer than ten, starting with *Highgate Ho!* and ending with *The Devil's Disciple*. Back at Highgate, an annual play became normal. *Julius Caesar* in 1943 was followed by Priestley's *Bees on the Boat Deck* the next year. *The Cholmeleian's* critic was cool. 'We must state candidly that Mr Priestley's *Bees on the Boat Deck* is a third-rate play.' However, he admitted that 'the "dramatis personae" (we cannot call them characters) were admirably cast' and that the Society was lucky to have the help of Kyffin Williams and his art department in producing a set under wartime conditions. The well deck of SS *Gloriana* cost just ten shillings.

During the following thirty years Kyffin Williams, a native of Anglesey and himself a distinguished painter, was to make a more important contribution to Highgate by his elevation of its art department. Among his pupils was the painter Patrick Procktor (1948–52) who later described himself as 'an ardent fan of Kyffin and very much influenced by his painting. He took us out to tea at the Copper Kettle after school', Procktor remembered, 'and to the Leicester Gallery – awakening to the world.'

War and the evacuation were clearly the central events of Bell's time, but these may eventually seem less significant than a change he brought to the nature of the school. Not everyone welcomed this. Twidell considered that he ran Highgate like a preparatory school. But the great majority understood and approved of Bell's policy which was based on his belief that 'the average boy is the most important boy in the school'.

112

PLATE 5

'The Old School House – entrance from Southwood Lane', a watercolour painted in 1833.

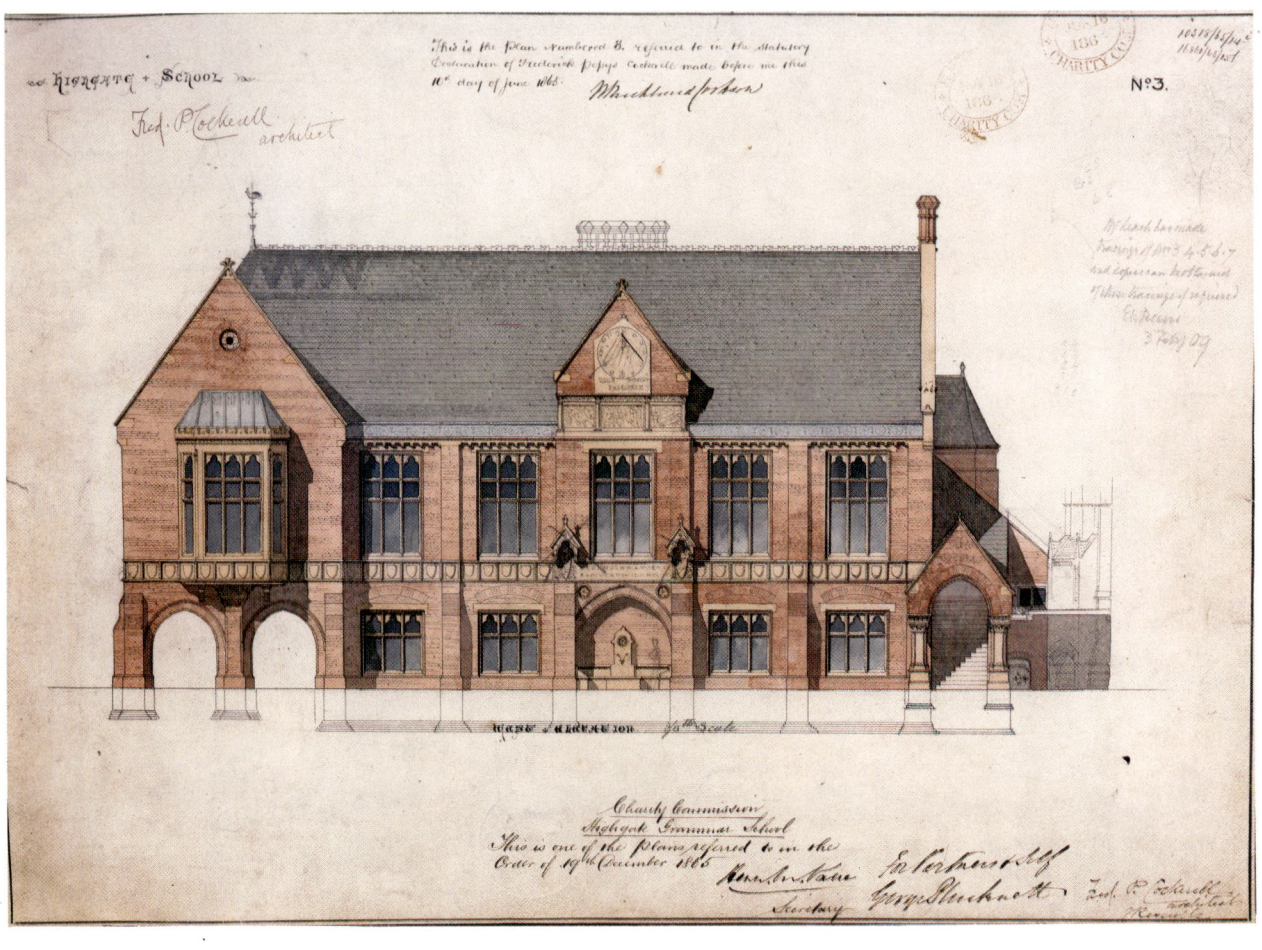

No. 3

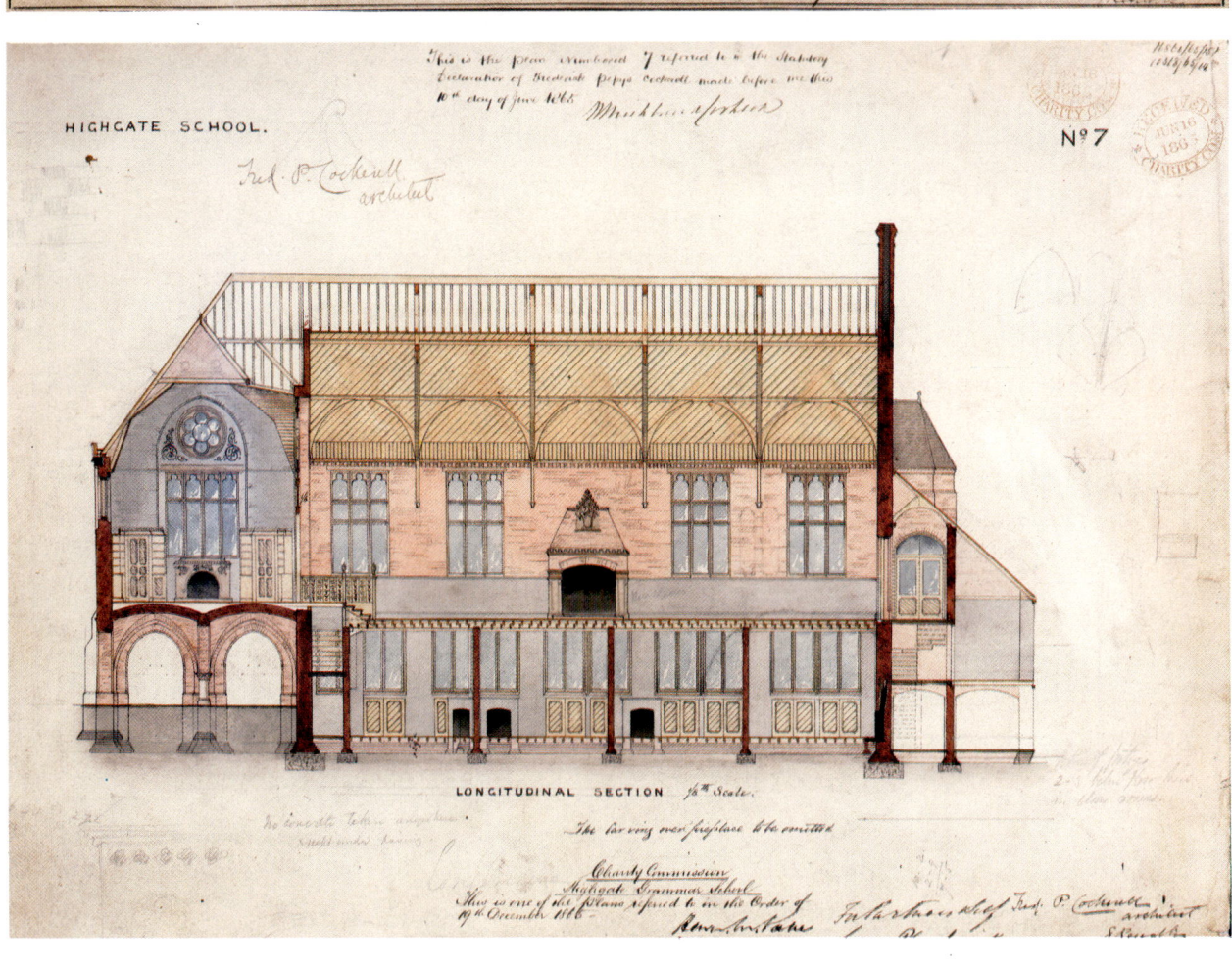

HIGHGATE SCHOOL
Fred. P. Cockerell architect

WEST ELEVATION ¼" Scale

No. 7

HIGHGATE SCHOOL.
Fred. P. Cockerell architect

LONGITUDINAL SECTION ¼" Scale

9

DOULTON SPANS THE 1960s
1955–1974

It is surprising, after Bell's liberalising regime, that his successor, Alfred John Farre Doulton, should have found Highgate an old-fashioned and authoritarian school; less so, perhaps, than Uppingham, his previous school, but 'the pattern was the same, with a formality in relations between staff and pupils, a prefectorial system with the power and the will to enforce discipline and as part of the discipline an insistence on minutiae over dress.' No boy, for example, was allowed to walk about the village with the bottom button of his jacket undone. Caps of varying significance were worn by ordinary boys, prefects and members of each school team.

It is a further irony that the boys considered Doulton essentially conservative. Students of the time were likely to take this view of any Head Master, but they had some justification. At his first Speech Day Doulton mentioned his surprise at discovering the previous April that 80 per cent of the candidates for admission were 'accustomed to watching television'. In his second term he abolished the Consultative Assembly, started by Bell, because he believed that it was undesirable for small boys to listen to the often radical and disrespectful opinions of seniors.

Doulton's position was not an easy one. While the country's boarding schools were mostly self-contained and isolated, Highgate, 'perched on its North London hill' was 'exposed to all the trendy winds that blow'. During the following years the growth of trendy unrest can be detected in *The Cholmeleian*. In May 1958 the editor warned readers that though he welcomed letters he would not be able to publish those which were violently anti-authoritarian. By January 1959 he, or his successor, had changed sides: 'There is more intelligence, life and general vitality in the School now than there has been for a long time, and perhaps with the disappearance of the staid, stale, self-satisfied Sixth Formers of today, the School may look forward to a not too inglorious five years or so.'

Alfred John Farre Doulton, Head Master 1955–74.

PLATE 6

Facing page: *West elevation and longitudinal section of Big School. Architect's plans dated 10 June 1865. Architect: F. P. Cockerill.*

113

Ivinghoe 'Expedition', 1956. TGM's 'Expeditions' were a great institution, enjoyed by many.

Some of this vitality took the form of wearing CND badges, an organisation with its headquarters at Finsbury Park which Doulton considered to have been 'infiltrated by extreme elements who used the movement as a stalking-horse for their designs'. When, however, Gibbon, now Second Master, told Doulton that they should be banned, Doulton retreated from confrontation, arguing that the school could hardly do so since it encouraged the wearing of Life-Saving badges, and furthermore it was 'preferable to know who had been bitten by the bug than to have this hidden'.

Inevitably London boys also began to imitate the fashions of the time, wearing winkle-pickers and growing their hair to their collars. Doulton maintained a conventional grey flannel suit as standard uniform: Michael Hammerson (1956–62) remembered Doulton's campaign against the wearing of the fashionable wide-bottomed trousers of the time. On the other hand he admitted that school caps looked absurd on top of flowing locks, and tactfully gave ground, allowing prefects to abandon them in 1967 and the rest of the Senior School in 1968. He showed the same sense of where it was wise to make concessions in 1969 when he restarted a modified form of consultative assembly, called the Sixth Form Council.

Soon after he arrived, the Suez affair was another disturbing external event, splitting Common Room, like the rest of the country, into opposing factions (Twidell remembered that Fox wouldn't speak to him for six months) and provoking four masters to write to *The Times* in protest against Britain's intervention. Unfortunately they wrote on Common Room paper, rousing the anger of the chairman of the Governors and of various Old Cholmeleians, but Doulton refused demands that they should be dismissed.

More generally, these were years when many boys rejected the notion of authority. But though Doulton admitted that a few boys refused to hold office when this was offered them, he claimed that there were 'always good candidates for office, and we had some sterling lads of quality among the Prefects and lesser officials'. One head boy saw Doulton's early years as those in which much that was traditional finally disappeared, in particular prefect power – power epitomised by the so-called long-walk which the head boy would make the full length of Big School on Speech Day, turning at the far end to face the assembled boys, imposing total silence throughout.

Doulton was more inclined to see the 1960s as a temporary phenomenon, and considered a confrontation he had with the Sixth Form in May 1970 as a final upsurge of anti-authoritarianism. This took the form of a threat to stage a demonstration during the school's match with the MCC, which, in the opinion of some Sixth Formers, had aligned itself with apartheid by not opposing that summer's South African cricket tour. The match was only four days away when Doulton, at an 8 a.m. meeting, persuaded the boys not to demonstrate.

In sum, Doulton's reactions to the events of the 1960s suggest that he was no encourager of change, but that, like a wise general, he knew when to abandon positions he could no longer hold. The essential thing, he believed, was to retain the boys' confidence and to do this he must always be prepared to listen to any serious point they wished to put to him.

At the same time that Doulton tried to protect the school from trendy winds, he consciously set about re-establishing the links with Highgate village which Johnston had neglected. The consequences were not always fortunate. When he allowed the girls of Channing School temporarily to take biology lessons at Highgate (since Channing had lost its senior biology mistress) he provoked 'a

Hubert Gibbon, staff 1922–65, teaching mathematics in characteristic stance, 1950s.

End of year prank, summer 1968: a dummy on the chapel roof. Head Master Doulton fourth from right in the foreground.

furore . . . . among my governors, one of whom charged me with starting to turn Highgate into a co-ed school'. But a friendly connection with Channing was established and before Doulton left its girls were performing alongside Highgate boys at school concerts.

The consequences of his accepting the invitation of the Conservative leader of Haringey Council to become an Alderman were more dramatic. On the council he suggested that the schools of the borough could be homogenised by bussing children from one area to another – a common practice in the USA. This involved commenting on the relative IQs of different races – a taboo subject. There was 'a huge furore and at its height the Chairman of the Education Committee and I left a Council meeting under police protection'. On the redbrick North Road wall of the school there appeared in large white letters the words DOULTON MUST GO – though whether put there by one of Highgate's New Commonwealth immigrants or one of its white middle-class remains uncertain.

The tomb of the poet Coleridge embroiled the school in an equally unwanted local conflict. It was sited below the west end of the chapel, where it had been left in 1867, this part of the new chapel being built on stilts above the old graveyard. In 1960 Ernest Raymond, author and literary critic, complained that the tomb had become derelict. The Governors did not deny this but maintained that the borough council was now responsible for the graveyard. Raymond and his supporters won the argument and in 1961 there was a ceremonial disinterring of Coleridge (at which the Poet Laureate, John Masefield, spoke) so that he could be reburied at St Michael's parish church. Some Old Cholmeleians considered that the school should not have surrendered its best-known corpse.

Less controversially, Doulton agreed to the Highgate Horticultural Society (of which the school doctor was the chairman) holding its summer exhibition in Big School. He became the Society's president and its later shows were held, as they still are, the Saturday after the end of term on Senior Field.

It was through music, however, that the school became most closely involved with the outside world. Music had been strong at Highgate since Wood and Cunningham Woods had done so much for it from the 1880s onwards, but it was the music master Edward Chapman (1928–62, a Northampton man with wide abilities, for two years commander of the Air Training Corps) who made it one of the school's best-known features. Before the war his enthusiasm had coincided with Bell's interest in music, and together they had introduced winter term recitals by such distinguished performers as the pianist Solomon. In Devon a house music competition had been started, which, like other Westward Ho! innovations, returned with the school to Highgate. In 1945 a new instrumental class was introduced – won with a Tchaikovsky piece played by the Lodge's ensemble of cornet, trombone, piano and drums.

After the war Chapman had reintroduced Friday afternoon recitals, which parents and villagers were invited to attend. Dennis Brain, Peter Pears and Benjamin Britten were among those who performed. And, in response to an appeal from Yehudi Menuhin (first president of the Highgate Society) the school allowed the Bath Festival Orchestra, which had lost its rehearsal room, to use

'War Requiem' programme and Benjamin Britten's congratulatory note to E. T. Chapman, Head of Music, and the boys of the school choir.

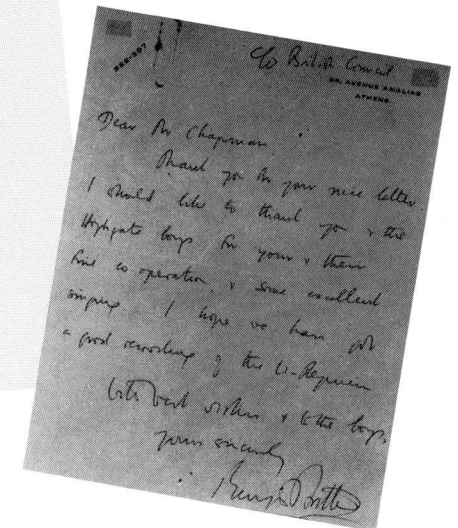

Big School, and then Dyne House, charging no fees on condition boys and masters could listen.

But it was the school's choir which, from the late 1940s onwards, acquired not merely a national but an international reputation, performing on the BBC (at the school's annual carol service), and at such continental festivals as Gelsenkirchen and Liège. Memorable choir performances were in Britten's *War Requiem* at the Albert Hall as the Choir of Angels, and in *Parsifal* at Covent Garden as the off-stage chorus. In 1958 it was the first school choir to sing at a Prom. The formation of the school chorus with about 200 members was, however, considered by Doulton the turning point, since it involved so many more boys in music. The chorus gave public performances of such major works as Handel's *Messiah* and Verdi's *Requiem*. Highgate's music and drama departments together staged *The Beggar's Opera* during the 400th anniversary celebrations of 1965. The composer, John Rutter, was one boy who came under Chapman's influence. Rutter considered Chapman a truly remarkable teacher, fired by an exceptional passion for music with which he infected his pupils. Though he was a disciplinarian, he never imposed his musical ideas, and the group of musicians who emerged from Highgate in the late 1950s and early 1960s are evidence of this. Besides Rutter they included John Tavener, a composer in a very different field, the concert pianist Howard Shelley, and David Cullen, an orchestrator for Andrew Lloyd Webber.

Chapman's outstanding qualities as a music teacher were balanced by an obstinacy which made him no easy man to work with. A succession of assistants came and went, only the last of them surviving more than two years. In the words of one colleague, 'his idea of compromise was getting his own way'.

In 1963 the school expanded its contacts with the outside world by starting a public service scheme, boys undertaking community work, first in Highgate, then in more distant parts of North London. Some decorated homes for the elderly, some taught immigrants to speak English, some taught disabled children to swim, one, Doulton remembered, wrote a letter for an old lady to her canary.

Henry IV, Part I, a 1957 school production.

Public service of this sort was required in order to obtain any higher medal than the Bronze in the Duke of Edinburgh Award Scheme, which the school joined after the Combined Cadet Force officially became voluntary in 1963.

For the Gold medal additional adventurous achievements were required of a sort which could not easily be arranged at Highgate. Fortunately the school had just bought Cerrig Pryfaid, a ruined farm in Snowdonia, at the suggestion of Kyffin Williams, who hoped his pupils would get artistic inspiration from his native mountains. 'In the early days,' wrote John Coombs, Second Master from 1981, 'a good few felt that a cottage in North Wales, 250 miles from Highgate, was a rather pointless addition to the school's properties. Very few who have been there will doubt the wisdom of that purchase ... Cerrig Pryfaid is more than a holiday cottage; it is a place where we have the opportunity ... to understand something of the motives and rewards of men who have faced the challenge of Everest or the North Wall of the Eiger, and to develop some of the skills, and self-reliance, which are needed to overcome the difficulties of this wild country.' In 1983, to celebrate the twentieth anniversary of the purchase of the farm, fifty boys spent a day climbing fifty peaks of over 2,000 feet, different groups climbing seven each, the whole party finally climbing Snowdon.

Doulton promoted another policy which helped to integrate village and school: the provision of flats in Highgate for masters. A total of six buildings, most of them in Bishopswood Road, were acquired or repossessed and converted. During the 1960s a number of veteran masters from before the war retired and the fact that he could offer accommodation to their replacements was, he believed, 'of prime importance in drawing good staff to Highgate'. Recruiting new masters, especially to teach mathematics, was not easy in these years. Of those whom Doulton appointed, though they had fewer than the usual qualifications, and who became outstanding teachers, he remembered in particular B. T. Bellis, later headmaster of Daniel Stewart's College, Edinburgh.

One master who eventually retired in Doulton's time was A. H. Fabian, an Old Cholmeleian who, in Johnston's time, had been almost as distinguished a games player as R. W. V. Robins. Returning to the school in 1932, he was for 25 years responsible for its many successes at cricket and soccer and its outstanding fives results. After 1947 Highgate and Eton were regular alternate winners of the Public School Eton Fives Competition. Between 1959 and 1974 Highgate won seven times. Fabian could be an alarming character, liable to turn puce with rage. Doulton remembered one such occasion, when he came to complain that boys had been stuffing the ink-wells of the desks in his classroom in the Dungeons with blotting-paper. Here Fabian taught one of the lower classes, for he was no intellectual, but he had unexpected talents, for example at after-dinner speaking. His own sporting career continued while he taught: in 1936 he played for Derby County in the semi-final of the FA Cup, and in 1937, 1939 and 1948 he won the Kinnaird Cup for Eton Fives with J. K. G. Webb, an Old Cholmeleian as his partner.

The event which, for a time, involved the school most closely with the village was the Highgate traffic scheme drama of 1962. The Ministry of Transport's proposal was to make Highgate Hill and High Street a one-way route for lorries from the docks to the north, while Archway Road would become a similar route for south-flowing traffic. The Minister, Ernest Marples, first told the Hornsey Borough Council of his plan in January, but the general public did not hear about it until 17 April. At once there was an outcry. As Doulton later pointed out, the issue was not purely a local one but involved an important principle. The minister was proposing a scheme which would benefit traffic, but failed to consider its wider social consequences.

On behalf of Highgate School and the six other schools which straddled the Highgate Hill route Doulton wrote a letter of protest to *The Times* (published on 2 May) and made Big School available for a public meeting attended by 700 people, who voted by a large majority against the scheme. On 7 May a more select meeting formed the Save Highgate Committee and on the 11th this appointed Doulton as its chairman.

During the next nine months the committee produced a long and a concise memorandum of protest, raised £1,184 for a fighting fund, collected 13,468 signatures to a petition, distributed 6,000 leaflets urging people to write to Marples, published and circulated a news sheet, *Voice of Highgate*, and held a further public meeting in Big School. 'The bulk of the important typing was done by the good Miss Bannister in the school offices,' Doulton wrote. 'Nearly all the foregoing took place in the course of a normal summer term.' Doulton acknowledged the debt he owed the school prefects at this time, when he was forced to 'desert the school a fair amount'. He also acknowledged the enormous debt the school owed Joan Bannister who for thirty-three years was in practice bursar as well as Head Master's secretary, and who was so totally involved with the school that she was offended when she was relieved of just one of her duties: the sending-out of bills to parents.

Eventually, on 26 January 1963 there came 'unheralded in a letter in my post at the school' the message that 'contrary to all expectations the Minister had decided not to proceed with the Lorry Route through Highgate ... Highgate rejoiced and that evening the Committee celebrated at School House.' The

Quatercentenary football match against an International XI – Jimmy Hill with the Highgate goal in his sights.

The new Dining Hall, 1958.

minister's subsequent decision to test out a one-way system which would circulate traffic round the school via Southwood Lane was described by Doulton as 'a nasty sting in the tail', by others as revenge. Subsequently the Committee became the Highgate Society, today one of the country's strongest local conservation societies.

There were important additions to the school's premises in these years. First came the new dining-hall, built at one side of Senior Field. Permission had been given for this in 1954, and as a result Bell had retired two years early, not wanting to take decisions about the design of such a major development which might not please his successor. It was fortunate, however, that the plan had been approved in principle when in 1955 Department of Education inspectors described the school's catering arrangements as 'archaic and unhygienic'. Less fortunately, its opening day coincided with the caterer's suicide, after Doulton had sacked him for inefficiency. The school doctor told Doulton that he owed his life to his failure to keep an appointment that morning with the man, who had planned to shoot Doulton first, then himself. Though the new hall helped to integrate day boys and boarders, its acoustics were a disaster. Junior and Senior Schools still dined as two sittings and while the seniors created a sustained roar, the noise of the juniors suggested 'an enormous aviary of little birds'.

Twelve years later (1970) came a covered swimming pool, built near the fives courts in one corner of Junior Field. This also opened with a misfortune, when too much chlorine was added to the water and those celebrating after their swim 'came to the supper with streaming eyes'.

Meanwhile, to celebrate the school's 400th anniversary in 1965, the Governors had launched an appeal to raise money for the most important new building since

Johnston's science block: Dyne House. This was erected in place of the building across Southwood Lane first bought for Dyne in 1845, then used by the Junior School as Cholmeley House from 1889 to 1938. The new Dyne House was to be a music and arts centre, and the first concert in its auditorium was given on 31 May 1967 by Yehudi Menuhin.

From the mid-1950s a threat hung over all independent schools: that they would be abolished by a Labour government. Doulton remembered a meeting of the Headmasters' Conference at which Robert Birley of Eton asked the shadow Education Secretary, Michael Stewart, 'Do you mean that a parent would be allowed to spend money he had legitimately earned on a sports car or a mink coat but not on his child's education?' 'That is precisely what I mean,' Stewart told him. But in practice the Labour government elected in 1964 left independent schools alone and concentrated on abolishing grammar schools.

First Labour Secretary for Education and Science was the Old Cholmeleian, Anthony Crosland. The following year Doulton remembered that 'as the Quatercentenary celebrations loomed up, the Press continually rang me to ask if [Crosland] would be attending the Governors' opening reception in Big School. I said they must ask the Minister, who remained silent until almost the last moment when a Secretary phoned to say that he was otherwise engaged. Shoddy,

Below left: *The old Dyne House, demolished 1966.*

Below: *E. T. Chapman and Yehudi Menuhin, KBE, opening the new Dyne House, 1967.*

nay ill-mannered, I thought ... Crosland's energies were directed elsewhere that year, to the production of Government Paper 10/65 which established comprehensive schooling as the pattern for secondary education throughout England and Wales.'

Doulton's flexible conservatism guided Highgate through its most difficult post-war years. To his staff he seemed an admirable Head Master. Benign, pipe-smoking, he wanted, in the words of Robert Read (who joined the staff in 1968) 'to create a family atmosphere'. Read remembered, as a young bachelor living in a room at the top of School House, sometimes coming in late and having to pass Doulton's bedroom on his way to his own attic room. The door would be open and Doulton, in bed with his wife, would call out good night.

Numbers alone are not a measure of a school's health, but they indicate a view taken of it by parents. During Doulton's time they rose steadily, from 870 (590 seniors, 280 juniors) to 980 (700 seniors, 280 juniors) in March 1974. More importantly, the school retained its academic standards, regularly securing many university awards and adopting such new teaching systems as the Mathematics in Education and Industry Scheme. Summing up Doulton's time, Norris Butcher, Second Master from 1976 to 1981, wrote, 'For many years under his guidance the school was a very happy and successful place.' The problems of the years which Doulton's regime spanned make such an assessment the more impressive.

Traffic has long been a problem in Highgate. Doulton's rallying of opposition to a proposed lorry route past the school led to the formation of the Highgate Society.

10

CALM AND CARE
1974–1989

'I ACTUALLY BELIEVE THAT in the end the sole purpose of being on earth is the worship of God.' So Roy Curtis Giles (who succeeded Doulton in 1974) told *The Cholmeleian* fifteen years later when he retired. Giles's religious convictions were a more important background to his Head Mastership than the conformist Christianity of many headmasters, and had consequences more significant than his introduction of twice weekly Communion services in the chapel. Though, as a linguist (for the previous four years Head of Modern Languages at Eton), he admitted to encouraging the rumour that he kept all fifty-three volumes of the Weimar edition of Goethe by his bed; the book he would have chosen for his desert island was the *Rule of St Benedict*.

Most apparent of the Benedictine qualities which he showed were humility and quietness. He would never run anywhere and hated any kind of rush. Though he took away armfuls of work to be done at home, his desk was always clear and he would seem to have infinite time for anyone who came to see him. It was his quietness which made him seem inscrutable, and there was a point beyond which even close friends did not penetrate. 'You never really knew what he was thinking,' said Peter Stone, appointed chaplain the year after Giles arrived and reputed to know him better than anyone else. 'He would have made an excellent poker player.'

But he was not really reserved, Stone considered. He had a penchant for making cutting remarks; he was an excellent mimic, picking on some characteristic and exaggerating it; and he was a relentless host, entertaining on average some 600 guests a year, many of them to 'old-fashioned dinner parties'. Mrs Giles 'liked to feel that the school flowed through their dining-room'. Giles saw himself, Stone believed, as an abbot, the school his community.

In his role as abbot it was likely that Giles would be enthusiastic about Highgate's 'elaborate and important system of pastoral care, which – I think

Roy Curtis Giles, Head Master 1974–1989 (left) and Jack Boreham, Old Cholmeleian and Governor, at the dedication of the memorial to Donald Spong, president of the Old Cholmeleian Society.

The centenary of the school's first Rugby football match, 16 March 1968.

– is much admired. I do think', he continued, 'that our day boy house system is unique. The way in which we try to divide them up by geographical areas, the way in which your housemaster goes and sees you at home.' He didn't pretend to know all the boys personally but claimed to know 'far more people than you think'. Others were convinced that he knew the names of every single boy. He would personally write the university references of some hundred boys each year, and, in the opinion of Robert Read (later Senior Master), 'had an amazing mind for summing up someone on paper'.

As for his staff, they never doubted that he would support them. Brian Spears, bursar in Giles's later years, remembered his regular Monday morning meetings with Giles – 'not the best time in the week for seeing your headmaster' – meetings from which he would invariably emerge feeling better. Furthermore Spears considered Giles an excellent administrator. There were 'not a lot of memos flying around' – Giles 'preferred to talk to you' – but things got done. If Spears ever remembered a mistake he had made he would feel sure that Giles would notice it.

Perhaps overambitiously, Giles considered that the school should stand for an older educational tradition, and that he had a mission to civilise not just the school but the less cultured people of the area. Though he refused to start a Parent Teachers' Association (which he believed encouraged disaffected minorities) he established an annual parents' forum – 'a sort of press conference' – at which he would answer questions and explain his aims for the school. It should not, he believed, aim to imitate 'a rugger-playing school like UCS'.

Perhaps unfortunately, personal quietness and modesty led to modesty about the school. He was not a publicist, and this affected not only the outside world's view of the school, but also the boys'. Michael Lindstrom, head of school in 1985, missed the sort of Assembly he had had at his previous school in South Africa where 'the achievements of the school were announced by the headmaster'. At Highgate some boys were simply unaware of the results of school matches.

Certainly Giles was not a games enthusiast. Questioned on the subject, he gave appropriate answers. 'Being part of a team is more important in sport than just playing as an individual. It teaches you something about the characters of those you play with.' And he would loyally appear on boundary or touch-line for every school match. But he would also observe that the English needed to invent cricket to give them a sense of eternity.

His lack of enthusiasm for games perhaps contributed to his poor relationship with Old Cholmeleians, but there was a more fundamental lack of sympathy. They sensed his disapproval of their nostalgic attitude to the school, considering that he failed to understand that this was an essential element in their continued connection with it, which could be exploited for its benefit. Certainly Giles considered that when it came to raising money, parents were more significant contributors, but he had a different explanation: Old Cholmeleians had not hated

The school chapel.

the school sufficiently – a sentiment which, with old boys of other schools, translated itself into loyalty.

Giles was also criticised for letting the academic standards of the school fall by accepting as boarders boys who were below standard in order to maintain boarding numbers. In response he claimed that, after he had closed Cordell, one of the four remaining boarding houses, he no longer automatically looked at the bottom stream to find boarders. On the other hand he believed that Highgate could save certain boys from Westminster, a 'sink or swim' school, where some might sink. Common Entrance was anyway 'a silly exam', and the school was right not to rely on its results, but sometimes take a few boys just below the pass mark who might blossom as boarders.

This should be remembered alongside Giles's observation, when addressing a dinner given in his honour by the Junior School and Senior School Common Rooms, that he did not consider it the role of a headmaster to *do* anything. David Williamson, Head of History, put it another way: 'Giles believed in organic growth'. Williamson remembered a time when classrooms were being reallocated and one group of masters wanted them to be grouped by subject, but another thought it more important that each day boy house should be given two classrooms for out-of-hours use. Giles refused to intervene but let the question be settled by Common Room vote.

The same was true, Read suggested, about the five day week, a question on which many masters had strong views. Read remembered taking the Common Room's eventual verdict to Giles and believed that it was that which led to the introduction of this important change. Giles remembered the process as far more complicated. At first he had felt that there was no need for a change, but had gradually been persuaded that the boys needed their Saturdays free. On the other hand there were many features of the school which he did not want it to lose – Saturday games for example. The whole question was considered by sub-committees of the masters who would have to make the new arrangement work, and the final decision, he claimed, had been a common one.

Whatever Giles's attitude to changes in the school's routine and organisation, there were additions and improvements to its premises during his time which were almost as important as those promoted by Doulton or Johnston. It was he who persuaded the Governors in 1976 to buy the Tabernacle, one of the most attractive as well as useful of today's buildings. In about 1758, a time when Nonconformist meeting places were forbidden within five miles of St Paul's, 'a Presbyterian Society, of some respectability', was established on the site of the Tabernacle. By the end of the century, however, its congregation was 'totally dissolved' and in 1806 the Unitarians, then in 1814 the Baptists acquired it. Some time between 1840 and 1860 the Baptists rebuilt it in today's form. Walking up Southwood Lane one day, Giles happened to see a 'For Sale' notice outside and was instantly convinced that it was a building the school must acquire, a conviction confirmed when he was shown round.

It cost the school a modest £17,000 to buy, but required a further £43,000 to repair, sums which were raised by disposing of Northfield Hall, the school's original gymnasium, and the sanatorium in Southwood Lane. At first the

The school library in the Tabernacle, a former dissenters' chapel, Southwood Lane.

Tabernacle was a Sixth Form centre, and it was formally opened for this purpose on 8 May 1978. But Giles – 'a great man for trusting boys' – was let down by them. More damage was done there than work and after seven years it was transformed into the library; few schools have so fine a library building.

The Tabernacle did nothing to solve the school's shortage of classrooms, and the sales of buildings by which it had been financed had virtually exhausted one way of providing for other developments. Furthermore at the time Giles arrived it was still in debt. During Doulton's time a loan of £100,000 had been obtained to pay for the dining hall, and this had been raised once more to the same figure when the appeal for Dyne House fell short by £85,000 of the building's cost. The covered swimming pool had also cost £62,000 more than allowed for, partly as a result of a disastrous thunderstorm at a critical moment during its building, and the excess had had to be met by a bank overdraft, an anonymous gift of £10,000 and loans from some ten individuals, Doulton included, of £5,000 each. These loans were repaid by mid-1975, but part of the overdraft and part of the original £100,000 loan were outstanding. For this reason, and because the school was no longer earning significant annual surpluses, the Governors and Giles decided that any substantial development would have to be financed by a new appeal. There had already been minor ones for conversion of Cordell into staff flats and for converting the Tabernacle. The new appeal was to be on a larger scale, and to be organised by a professional fund-raiser. It was launched in 1981, with a target (which it successfully raised) of £500,000, its principal purpose to provide a new block of mathematics classrooms. This was to face North Road, as a northerly extension of the Science Building. Early in 1983 it was opened by Lord Garner, an Old Cholmeleian, Chairman of the Governors for the previous seven years, and given his name as the Garner Building. Its usefulness apart, its classrooms provide some fine views over distant London.

The Garner Building, opened in 1983, provided first rate new classrooms for mathematics and computing.

Less obvious than the Garner Building was a systematic refurbishing of the school's remaining boarding houses, which had come to seem primitive by the standards of the day. Their large dormitories were transformed into smaller ones, with no more than eight beds each for Third and Fourth Form boys, and into study bedrooms for Fifth and Sixth Form boys.

The appeal of 1981 had been intended to fund other developments, including the conversion of the Senior School gymnasium (on the slope below Dyne House) into 'a much larger sports area'. But that idea was abandoned and a new appeal was launched for the building of a sports centre which would incorporate the covered swimming pool at the corner of the Junior Field. The Mallinson Sports Centre, named after Theodore Mallinson, included indoor cricket nets, fencing pistes, arrangements for javelin and discus throwing, weight-training, a gym for volley ball or badminton and a refreshment room. It cost £2,000,000 (to which the appeal contributed £575,000) and is one of the school's major assets.

By this time Mallinson himself, besides being the school's Record Keeper, had become a roving ambassador for the Friends of Highgate School Society. On a trip in 1980 he travelled 26,000 miles in five weeks, attending eleven Old Cholmeleian reunions – in South Africa, Australia, New Zealand and California. Among those he met was Colin Dryborough, one-time captain of

PLATE 7

Left: *School football XI, 1885.*

Below: *A century later, a cricket match on Senior Field with School House in the background.*

PLATE 8

Right: *An aerial view of the school, looking across Southwood Lane and North Road towards Kenwood.*

Left: *An art class in the courtyard below Dyne House.*

Middlesex cricket, now living in Perth. In 1989 the school celebrated a double event: Mallinson's eightieth birthday, and his fifty years at Highgate School. A book of essays, entitled *T.G.M.*, on the school and related subjects, was published in his honour.

The Friends of Highgate, who partly sponsored Mallinson's world tour, had been founded in 1945, with the main aim of helping financially with the education at Highgate of the sons of Old Cholmeleians who had died or retired. These were at first likely to be sons of those killed in the war and the Friends were in practice supporting a War Memorial Fund. By 1991 they had capital (including large bequests from three Old Cholmeleians, E. E. Chipp, C. C. Griffith and C. G. Baker) of £900,000 and were assisting forty boys. The need for such assistance grows and though at first all requests were accepted, in recent years some have had to be refused.

One of the less expected results of the five-day week and abolition of Saturday school was that more boys were able to come from Jewish families. There had been an earlier influx of Jews in wartime as a result of German persecution, and the Jewish Circle had been formed at Westward Ho! to hold regular Friday meetings. In recent years boys have begun to come not only from Greek Orthodox homes but from Hindi and Muslim ones. There have also for many years been Catholic boys. In 1992 in the Senior School there were 300 Church of England boys, 48 Roman Catholic, 35 Greek Orthodox, 120 Jewish, 30 Hindu, 28 Muslim and 14 from other religious backgrounds. For the other non-Christians there are weekly meetings in Dyne House where religious, moral and social problems are discussed. Such a development might have embarrassed an

Theodore Mallinson unveiling the plaque honouring T. S. Eliot (member of staff) and John Betjeman (pupil at the Junior School), 1987.

Anglican foundation but the school considers that the new mixture is the opposite of a problem since all boys gain from contact with others from different ethnic and religious backgrounds. In 1991–92 Sushil Shah, whose parents were Indians from Kenya, was head of school.

On the other hand Giles believed that the school should keep faith with its original founder's intentions and retain its essentially Anglican character. In particular he considered that the Junior School had become secularised – it called its annual carol service, for example, a carol concert. One thing which had attracted him to Highgate was its chapel, a rare feature at London schools. He wanted boys as they arrived from North Road, not automatically to turn their attention to the school buildings to their left, but at least to be conscious of the chapel to their right. He hoped to bring religion back into the centre of school life, and would show parents the triptych high above the entrance to Big School with boys at work, at play *and* at prayer. It was not a change to be made easily. The front cover of *The Cholmeleian* for October 1982 showed a school version of snakes and ladders, square 74 marked CAUGHT SINGING HYMNS IN CHAPEL – START AGAIN.

Summing up his view of Highgate, Giles considered that its boys were professional schoolboys: they expected a good job to be done by them, and provided the school did this they would keep their side of the bargain. In his time he believed that the partnership worked well.

11

TODAY AND TOMORROW
1989–1993

NEWLY APPOINTED HEADMASTERS often consider that the school they have inherited is in need of reform. Richard Paul Kennedy, who succeeded Giles in 1989, was no exception. Grandson of a miner, nine times a sprinter in Great Britain's athletics team, Kennedy had taught at Shrewsbury and Westminster, then for five years had been Deputy Headmaster at Bishop's Stortford College. Over the previous fifteen years Highgate's numbers had fallen by 100 and, in his opinion, the curriculum needed to be brought up to date.

On the other hand Highgate's situation, buildings and playing fields gave it enormous potential. Though mainly a day school and therefore relatively less expensive, it could provide many of the traditional features which parents associated with boarding public schools.

During the last few years the Governors have been pleased by Kennedy's exploitation of this potential. In the Chairman's view it is the duty of a headmaster, as the equivalent of the chief executive of a company, to be the technical and managerial expert who brings to his board the latest ideas in education, and who puts into effect with efficiency decisions on change which the Governors agree and which the school can afford. Kennedy has satisfied them in both these ways.

One of his earliest innovations was the appointment, when the Second Master retired, of a Deputy Head Master from outside the school, to be supported by a Senior Master from the Common Room. The Deputy Head Master was to be a young man, probably due to become a headmaster as Kennedy himself had done, with whom the Head Master could discuss plans and policy. He would help with an examination of what the school was, where it should be going and how it should get there. He would also be responsible for the school's academic curriculum and standards.

Kennedy did not share Giles's reluctance to publicise the school, making the

Richard Paul Kennedy, shown here in discussion with school prefects, was appointed Head Master in 1989.

The school's William Wawn defends on First Club in front of School House. Captain of the Old Cholmeleians, Paul Maidment, looks on.

most of what the *Hampstead and Highgate Express* called 'a coup' within a few months of arriving when the Education Secretary, John MacGregor accepted the Governors' invitation to open the Mallinson Sports Centre. MacGregor had had a son in the school, and his wife was a Governor.

The Sports Centre made possible another development by freeing the boys' changing room building at the opposite side of Junior Field for transformation into the Richards Music Centre. At the cost of £400,000 this has provided the Junior School with a building it has long needed. David Richards, an Old Cholmeleian, Chairman of the Governors since 1983, was present on 28 April 1992 when another Old Cholmeleian, the composer John Rutter, formally opened the building. On the same occasion Allan Fox, Master of the Junior School, reminded guests that it was he and Giles who had originally conceived the freeing of the old changing rooms for their transformation.

Kennedy and the Governors promoted a number of other developments which they considered to be urgently needed, first of these being improvements to the dining hall with its bare floor, fixed sittings and deafening sound effects. At the cost of £300,000 this was refurbished, given new kitchens and redesigned for self-service meals. Some had argued that the new arrangements would have disadvantages: masters and boys would no longer lunch and converse together; the Head Master would no longer be daily exposed to the whole school. But in most ways the new arrangements civilised school lunches, and the Head Master even began to receive letters of praise about school food.

Soon there were more changes. The Lodge, one of the three remaining boarding houses, was closed, and in 1992 Grindal followed. Again there were misgivings amongst old members of Grindal, a house with so many sporting traditions. Now only School House remained for weekly boarders. Though the

TODAY AND TOMORROW

closures were a consequence of the decline in demand for boarding places (not only at Highgate but at many other schools) they required a deliberate decision to stop trying to maintain boarding houses if they had to be filled with boys below the standard set for day boys.

At the same time it was announced that a Pre-Preparatory School for 3- to 7-year-olds would be opened in 1993, using Grindal as its building. It would have places for 120 boys or girls, but this (to the disappointment of a few parents) would imply no plan to admit girls to the Junior or Senior Schools. Its aim was to respond to parental demand, especially from working mothers, for a top-grade start to their children's schooldays, and to offer continuity in the education of boys, from kindergarten to A-level.

By 1993 further changes had followed: the redesign of the offices around the Head Master's study, the conversion of the space below the north end of Big School into an undercroft meeting-room, the refurbishing of the Senior Pavilion, the conversion of the Lodge into flats, and the important conversion of Field House, extending the facilities of the Junior School as it expanded to 370 pupils. With the exception of the Pre-Preparatory School, these costly developments were all financed from the school's current income and reserves.

All was threatened by the general election of 1992. If the Labour party had

Junior School boys, summer 1989.

won the Chairman would have called an emergency meeting of the Governors and asked them to reconsider all the capital projects they had agreed. Abolishing the charitable status of independent schools would have had less effect on Highgate than on better-endowed schools. It was Labour's plans to increase substantially taxes on higher earners – exactly those who formed the great majority of Highgate's parents – which would have seriously altered the school's prospects. One Old Cholmeleian, Jonathan Hill (1973–8), was John Major's Political Secretary. Old Cholmeleians were not, however, unanimously Conservative. Charles Clarke (1963–8) was expected to be the man who would run Neil Kinnock's Downing Street kitchen cabinet.

Other changes of the last few years have been intended to improve Highgate's scholastic standing. Kennedy considered the Common Room to be middle-heavy, with only two masters in their twenties; his early appointments were aimed at correcting the balance. He also believed that Highgate had fallen behind in the teaching of science and technology. Today all pupils in the Junior and Senior Schools study information technology.

The school's intake could not be improved so simply, and Kennedy anyway believed that Highgate 'should not be an academic hothouse'. Nevertheless he set out to enhance the quality of the boys it attracted by cultivating preparatory schools and bringing Highgate's entry system into line with its rivals. His aim was to make Highgate a first choice for parents, not a school they could fall back on if their sons failed to get into Westminster or St Paul's. A higher academic standard for entry, far from reducing demand, has had the opposite effect, numbers soon rising to those of Doulton's last years and to 1,000 by 1994.

Kennedy looks ahead with confidence to Highgate's future, but without rigid

The annual cross-country race on Hampstead Heath passes Kenwood House, 1991.

Richard Kennedy and boys, the Daily Telegraph, *September 1991.*

ideas about the form this will take. A school like Highgate must be prepared to adapt itself to what is required of it. It must convince parents that it is worth what it costs them, and though this may become more difficult, at present, with a waiting-list which enables the school to set a high standard for entry, it is clearly doing so.

In its first four and a quarter centuries 'The free Grammar School of Sir Roger Cholmeley, Knight' at Highgate has passed through many transformations. First, steady decline for 250 years into a school for the poorest boys of the village, then reprieve as a grammar school with Lord Eldon's famous verdict of the 1820s. Dyne, who must still be reckoned the school's greatest Head Master, exploited the opportunity this provided; under him and his two nineteenth-century successors it climbed steadily into the ranks of the country's foremost public schools.

Under Johnston in the first half of the twentieth century Highgate not only led the country in introducing the teaching of relevant science and technology, but in the late 1920s was on the verge of another great step; now that half its pupils were boarders it seemed about to become the sort of boarding public school that other major schools, including its neighbour Harrow, had long been. If the Depression which abruptly reversed this development appeared at the time a misfortune, today it can be seen as fortunate, since Highgate's future as a day school is turning out to be more likely to give it a bright future.

When another war followed, partial evacuation from London seemed to threaten the school's future, but again it survived, and survived also the social upheavals of the 1960s.

These events must be remembered when, today, the school seems to face challenges which are as great or greater than those of any other time. If our view of these is distorted by their closeness, they are undoubtedly formidable. On the one hand there are the nationwide changes to the structure of education which have reached individual schools in the shape of the National Curriculum and other government-inspired initiatives, on the other are the changes to the nature of rival schools, in particular the arrival of the opted out state school which may present an independent school like Highgate with new and challenging competition.

Parallel to such educational matters are social changes which are also setting fresh problems. The competition between reading and television does not decrease. The parents who traditionally sent their children to public schools (mostly of the professional classes) are not becoming richer, indeed relatively less so. Single parents — today more and more numerous — are finding independent education for their children especially costly. On top of all this schools must find ways of handling drugs, AIDS and street violence, perhaps the biggest fears of parents bringing up children in London today.

Difficult as such problems may seem, the fact that Highgate has survived for more than four centuries is reassuring. So, too, is its thriving state today, and even more so the confidence of its Governors and Head Master that it is the sort of school which can combine old public school traditions with features which today's London parents want.

Without doubt the many transformations it has undergone would make today's Highgate School barely recognisable to its founder, but Sir Roger Cholmeley was nothing if not a pragmatist, and there are good reasons for thinking that — mixed with astonishment — he would feel pleasure and pride in what he discovered.

SELECTED LIST OF OLD CHOLMELEIANS

NICHOLAS ROWE (1686) Poet Laureate.

EDMUND YATES (1840) Journalist and author; chose 'Lewis Carroll' as pen-name of Charles Dodgson.

RICHARD BETHELL (1842) Baron Westbury.

SLINGSBY BETHELL (1842) Barrister; Clerk of Committees, House of Lords.

GEORGE CRAWLEY (1842) Railway builder.

SIR JOHN DONNELLY (1843) Major General; Permanent Secretary, Department of Education and Science.

SIR RICHARD RIVINGTON HOLMES (1843) Archaeologist, author and artist.

R. S. ROBERTSON (1845) Major General, Indian Mutiny.

BENJAMIN ROGERS (1845) Author, first Old Cholmeleian to become President of the Oxford Union Society.

E. L. JERVIS (1845) Major, 13th Lt Dragoons, siege of Sebastopol and charge at Balaclava.

CANON HENRY VENN (1846) Canon of Canterbury.

THE REVEREND DR JOHN VENN (1846) President of Caius College, Cambridge.

EDWARD ATKINSON (1848) Electrician and aeronaut.

JOHN BRADLEY DYNE (1848) Barrister; Treasurer and Chairman of the Governors, 1906–09.

THOMAS CLARKE TATHAM (1849) Barrister; Treasurer and Chairman of the Governors, 1909–14.

PROFESSOR W. W. SKEAT (1850) Etymologist.

PHILIP WORSLEY (1851) Translator.

SIR CHARLES MURRAY (1853) MP.

GERARD MANLEY HOPKINS (1854) Poet.

SIR E. W. N. KNOCKER (1854) Solicitor; Registrar of the Cinque Ports.

THOMAS PRICE (1854) MP.

SIR EDWARD PEMBERTON LEACH (1856) General; Victoria Cross.

MARCUS CLARKE (1858) Australian author of *For the Term of His Natural Life*.

E. H. COLERIDGE (1858) Editor of *Letters of S. T. Coleridge*.

SIR JOHN LEACH (1858) Major General.

CHARLES CHURCH (1859) Barrister; Treasurer and Chairman of Governors, 1920–9.

PROFESSOR W. H. PIKE (1859) Chemist.

EDWARD BICKERSTETH (1860) Bishop of Japan.

R. G. WARTON (1860) England cricket team manager.

HAROLD PEMBERTON LEACH (1861) Brigadier General.

SIR EDWARD BEAUCHAMP (1862) Bt., MP, Chairman of Lloyds.

A. F. Leach (1862) Historian.

Walter Scrimgeour (1862) Stockbroker.

A. J. Jukes Browne (1863) Geologist and author.

Sir Reginald Blomfield (1865) Architect.

Sir John Cockburn (1865) Premier of South Australia.

R. C. Lehmann (1865) MP, first editor of *The Cholmeleian,* later editor of *The Daily News* and *Punch.*

T. C. Porter (1865) Brigadier General.

Sir Robert Price (1866) MP.

Sir W. H. Roberts (1866) Judge.

Dr Samuel Bickersteth (1867) Chaplain to the King.

Dr E. G. Hardy (1867) Principal of Jesus College, Oxford.

Richard Norton (1867) Baron Grantley.

Sir Charles Thomas-Stanford (1868) Bt., MP.

W. L. A. Bartlett (1868) MP and philanthropist, married Angela Burdett-Coutts.

C. A. E. Pollock (1870) President of Corpus Christi College, Cambridge.

Sir Michael Rimington (1870) Lieutenant General; HQ Staff, Indian Cavalry Corps.

Sir Archibald Bodkin (1871) Director of Public Prosecutions.

F. G. M. Rowley (1875) Brigadier General.

Sir Frederic Gordon (1876) Major General.

William Alderson (1878) Vice Admiral.

Professor F. L. Griffith (1878) Egyptologist.

Sir William Horwood (1879) Brigadier General; Chief Commissioner, Metropolitan Police.

Sir Charles Robertson (1880) Principal and Vice-Chancellor of Birmingham University.

Sir Stanley Tubbs (1881) Bt., MP.

Sir Charles Batho (1882) Lord Mayor of London.

H. B. Durrant (1883) Bishop of Lahore.

Lord Justice Mackinnon (1883).

E. H. M. Waller (1883) Bishop of Madras.

Sir Percy Mackinnon (1884) Chairman of Lloyds.

H. G. Pellissier (1885) Composer and satirist.

Ernest Greenwood (1886) Attorney General, Northern Nigeria.

Sir Maurice Gwyer (1887) Chief Justice of India.

Sir A. G. Tansley (1887) Botanist; Chairman of Nature Conservancy Council.

C. C. Walker (1887) Aeronautical engineer.

W. G. Hardie (1889) Archbishop of the West Indies.

Sir Roger Gaskell Hetherington (1889) President of the Institution of Civil Engineers; Treasurer and Chairman of Governors, 1929–44.

A. L. Kitching (1889) Bishop of Uganda.

N. H. Tubbs (1890) Bishop of Rangoon and of Chester.

N. Standfast (1890) Died on *Lusitania.*

Sir Frank Alexander (1892) Lord Mayor of London.

Reverend E. H. Thorold (1894) Chaplain to the King.

Herbert Edmunds (1895) President of the Royal Philatelic Society.

H. M. Wood (1895) International lawyer, League of Nations.

R. D. Robertson (1897) Rugby Union for Scotland.

A. S. Quartermaine (1900) Chief engineer, Great Western Railway; President of Institution of Civil Engineers.

P. D. Hepworth (1902) Principal Architect, Commonwealth War Graves Commission.

V. H. Galbraith (1904) Regius Professor of Modern History, Oxford.

Stephen Longrigg (1905) Brigadier; Treasurer and Chairman of the Governors, 1954–65.

Sir Geoffrey Shakespeare (1905) Bt., MP, Private Secretary to David Lloyd George, Chief Whip of Liberal Party and Minister for Overseas Trade.

SELECTED LIST OF OLD CHOLMELEIANS

Gordon Crole-Rees (1905) Davis Cup tennis player.

Sir Christopher Andrewes (1908) Researcher into typhus and influenza.

W. R. Seagrove (1909) Great Britain Olympic athlete.

Harald Melvill (1910) Actor and author.

G. W. Walker (1910) Director of Beaulieu Motor Museum and BBC motor-cycling commentator.

D. G. Sadler (1911) Inventor of the Magnetic Mine Sweep and novelist.

J. P. Hosford (1912) Professor, Royal College of Surgeons.

A. D. Bush (1912) Composer and pianist.

Roland Culver (1914) Actor.

Sir Robert Scott (1914) Governor of Mauritius.

Professor D. C. Harrison (1915) Biochemist.

Lord Bowles (1915) MP and Deputy Chairman of Labour Party.

Sir Alexander Valentine (1915) Chairman of London Transport.

T. S. Eliot (staff 1916) Poet and playwright, Order of Merit.

Sir Guy Sayer (1916) Vice Admiral.

C. W. Sheldon (Schoedelin) (1916) Director General of Courtaulds, South Africa.

Douglas Lowe (1917) QC; twice Olympic 800m. gold medalist; President of the Bar Council; Treasurer and Chairman of Governors, 1965–76.

E. O. D. Keown (1917) Drama critic and 'Eric' of *Punch*.

Alan Blumlein (1918) Inventor and radar pioneer, with 128 patents in electronics and telecommunications.

Sir Anthony Plowman (1918) Judge.

Kenneth Clements (1919) Bishop of Canberra and Goulburn.

E. J. Tickell (1919) Novelist, screenwriter and biographer.

Lord Garner (1920) Diplomat Treasurer and Chairman of Governors, 1976–83

Sir John Betjeman (1919) Poet Laureate and author.

Sir Harold Beeley (1921) Diplomat.

A. H. Fabian (1921) England Amateur Footballer; FA amateur Cup finalist with Corinthian Casuals; FA Cup semi-finalist with Derby County.

L. V. Grinsell (1921) Archaeologist.

Philip Harben (1921) Chef.

Alexander King (1921) Chemist.

R. W. V. Robins (1921) England cricketer, 1930–8; Captain of Middlesex CCC.

Roger Le Geyt Hetherington (1921) President of the Institution of Civil Engineers.

Sir Anthony Selway (1921) Air Marshal.

J. N. CHAUDHURI (1923) Major General; Military Governor of Hyderabad.

SIR ARTHUR HETHERINGON (1924) Chairman of British Gas Corporation.

DR ROBERT STOPFORD (staff 1924) Bishop of Peterborough, London and Bermuda.

W. H. WEBSTER (1924) President of MCC and England amateur footballer.

SIR MARTIN FURNIVAL-JONES (1925) Director General of the Security Service (MI5).

E. P. YOUNG (1926) Author of *One of Our Submarines is Missing*.

SIR JAMES LINDSAY (1928) Industrialist and management consultant.

PROFESSOR AUSTYN MAIR (1929) Aeronautical engineer.

ANTHONY CROSLAND (1931) MP, Secretary of State for Education and Science and Foreign Secretary.

SIR ALAN NEALE (1931) Permanent Secretary.

SIR GEOFFREY ELLERTON (1932) Civil servant in Kenya, Chairman of Local Government Boundary Commission for England.

ALEXANDER COMFORT (1933) Physician, poet and novelist.

JOHN BOX (1934) Film production designer – winner of eight British and American Academy awards.

LORD ACKNER (1934) Judge and Law Lord.

DENIS ALLPORT (1935) Industrialist.

SIR RONALD GRIERSON (1935) Industrialist.

SIR BRIAN NEILL (1935) Lord Justice of Appeal.

COLIN TURNER (1935) MP.

SIR ROBERT CLARK (1936) Solicitor and company chairman.

HENRY FAIRLIE (1936) Journalist and broadcaster.

RAYMOND ANDREWS (1938) Present of the Architectural Association.

R. G. BAYLIS (1938) Rear Admiral.

STANLEY BOOTH-CLIBBORN (1938) Bishop of Manchester.

D. G. TITFORD (1938) Rear Admiral.

H. G. WOODS (1938) Major General.

GERARD HOFFNUNG (1939) Cartoonist, impresario and author.

JUAN LUGO (1939) Spanish diplomat.

STUART MACLURE (1939) Editor of *Times Educational Supplement* and author.

SIR PATRICK NEILL (1939) Warden of All Souls College and Vice-Chancellor of Oxford University.

GEOFFREY PALMER (1939) Actor.

JOHN GOBLE (1941) Solicitor.

SELECTED LIST OF OLD CHOLMELEIANS

CHRISTOPHER MORAHAN (1941) Theatre, television and film director.

GUY BARNETT (1942) MP.

DAVID RICHARDS (1942) President of the Institute of Chartered Accountants; Treasurer and Chairman of Governors, 1983 –

WALLY OLINS (1943) Designer.

MICHAEL WELBANK (1944) Architect and President of the Royal Town Planning Institute.

KYFFIN WILLIAMS (staff 1944) RA, artist.

BARRY NEWTON (1945) Air Vice Marshal; gentleman usher to HM The Queen.

PROFESSOR ROY GOODE (1946) Lawyer.

PAUL MANOUSSO (1946) Architect and artist.

BARRY NORMAN (1946) Film critic and author.

CARL PINI (1946) Violinist.

ROBIN RAY (1947) Broadcaster, actor and author.

EDWARD FIELD (1948) Diplomat.

PATRICK PROCKTOR (1948) RWS, painter, etcher, illustrator and stage designer.

MARTIN GILBERT (1949) Churchill's biographer.

ANTHONY CAMDEN (1950) Oboeist and conductor.

A. N. CARLIER (1950) Major General, Royal Engineers.

COLIN DRYBOROUGH (1951) Cricketer, captain of Middlesex CCC.

SIR MALCOLM FIELD (1951) Company chairman.

ANTHONY GREEN (1951) RA, painter.

ADRIAN LYNE (1953) Film director.

J. S. F. BOWAN (1954) Australian diplomat.

SIR CLIVE SINCLAIR (1954) Inventor.

ROBERT BURNS (1956) British Ambassador to Israel.

JOHN TAVENER (1957) Composer.

ROBERT ATKINS (1958) MP; Minister for Sport and Northern Ireland Office Minister.

MIKE OCKRENT (1958) Theatre director.

JOHN RUTTER (1958) Composer.

Old Cholmeleians who entered the school after 1960 are omitted from this list.

INDEX

Adam, Robert 29
Abbey News, The 106
Adey Frank 73–4
Aguirre, L. 95
Allcock, Rev Arthur Edmund 71–80, 82; building of Central Hall 74–5; character and appearance 71, 73; encouragement of games 70; organisation of day boy houses 71; reorganisation of forms 74; resignation 80; teaching 80
Amsterdam 98
Anglesey 12
Arthur, Prince 63
Arnold, Dr Thomas 46, 50
Ashridge House 10
Ashurst House, Highgate 26
Atterbury, Dr Lewis 24, 25, 33
Australia 128
A.Z. *see* Domville, William

Balliol College, Oxford 99
Bannister, K. Joan 106, 119
Barfield, Arthur 92, 93
Bateman, Philip 102, 108
Bayley, Thomas 94–5
Beaumont, E. 59
Bees on the Boat Deck 112
Beggar's Opera, The 117
Belcher, William 38
Belgium 56
Bell, Geoffrey Foxall 96, 99–112, 113, 116; admiration of Kurt Hahn 99; appointment 99; character and career 99; policy 112; preparation for war 101; promotion of societies 99; removal of Junior School 100; resignation 120
Bell, Mrs Geoffrey 99, 110
Bell, Canon George Charles 63
Bellis, B. T. 118
Bennet, Revd Thomas 34, 35, 38
Berlin 98
Best Poems of John Betjeman, The 94
Betjeman, John 93–4, 129
Bickersteth, Bishop Edward 177
Birley, Robert 121
Bisham House, Highgate 14
Bishop's Stortford College 131
Black Book, The, of Lincoln's Inn 10
Blomfield, Sir Reginald 87
Bloomsbury 29
Bloxham, Charles John 51, 59
Bloxham, William 49
Bodkin, Revd W. D. 60, 66, 67

Boer War 76–7
Boreham, Jack 123
Boy's Own Paper 91
Brasenose College, Oxford 21, 53, 59
Brief Account of the Free Grammar School, A 41
Britten, Benjamin 117
Bromwich, William 32
Brougham, Lord 41
Brown, Thomas 21
Browne, Revd John 21–4; appointment 21; copying of statutes 22; salary 24
Buck, Geoffrey 90–1
Buenos Aires 81
Bullin, Edward 110
Burnie, A. E. 73
Burrows, E. 76
Butcher, Norris 122
Bute, Third Earl of 29
Butterfield 53
Butler, Bishop Samuel William 46

Calcutta 81
California 128
Cambridge University 98, 104
Canada 99
Cape Town 81
Carter, Dr Thomas 21, 21
Cartwright, Mr 105–6
Causton, Revd T. H. 47
Chadwick, William 13
Chamberlain, Neville 100, 101
Champneys, Revd Weldon 34
Channing School 115
Chapman, Edward T. 116–17
Chariots of Fire 97
Charity Commissioners 64, 75
Charle, Johnson 17, 18
Charles II 21
Charterhouse 53–4, 61
Cheltenham College 47
Child, Lady 23
Cholmeleian, The 56, 58, 59, 60, 64, 66, 68, 70, 72–3, 75, 76, 85, 105, 111, 112, 113, 123
Cholmeley, Hugh 19
Cholmeley, Jasper 12, 14, 17, 19
Cholmeley, Sir Richard 10
Cholmeley, Sir Roger 8, 9–19, 40, 41, 42, 43, 135–6
Christ's College, Cambridge 21
Christ's Hospital 99
Churchill, Sir Winston 104

City of London School 54, 101, 109
Clarendon Commission 53
Clarke, Charles 134
Clarke, J. P. H. 59
Clifton College 46, 47, 61, 71
Coleridge, Samuel 35, 116
Comic Times 49
Coombs, John 118
Cooper, W. D. C. 46
Cordell, Sir William 17–18
Cotton, Bishop George 46
Crawford, G. R. 70
Crich, Miss 78, 80
Cricketer, The 97
Crosland, Anthony 121–2
Crawley, George Abraham 50, 51, 56
Crawley, George Baden 56–7
Crawley, Robert Townsend 56
Cullen, David 117
Czechoslovakia 101, 11

Dalston 78, 86
Daniel Stewart's College 118
Dartington Hall 107
Dartmoor 103, 111
de Beaumont, A. R. 60, 62–3
Delhi 77
Description of England 9
Desoutter, Marcel 91
Deutsch, W. D. 107
Devon 101–7, 116
Dictionary of National Biography 29
Dienes, S. P. 107
Dodgson, Charles 49
Domville, William 15, 42
Doulton, Alfred John Farre 106, 113–22, 123, 127; alderman 116; career and character 113; opinion of school 113; opposition to traffic scheme 119–20. relationship with village 115–20
Douton, Revd G. W. 80, 92, 93
Dryborough, Colin 128
Dulwich College 68
Dumaresq, Onfrey William 106
Dyne, Dr John Bradley 45–60, 71, 75, 107, 135; appearance 61; appointment 46; concern with academic standards 47–8; earnings 60; leaving presents 60; loans to school 49, 51, 59; popularity/unpopularity 58–9; resignation 59–60
Dyne, John Bradley, jnr 60

Edward VI 9, 10, 14, 16

INDEX

Edwards, John 26, 27, 30, 31
Eiger 118
Eldon, Lord Chancellor 13, 15, 43–4, 45, 135
Elizabeth, Queen 10, 11, 12, 14, 16, 18, 45
Eliot, T. S. 93–4, 129
Elmdon Grammar School 28
Elms, The, Highgate 56
Elton, Revd W. H. 60
Endowed Schools Commission 64
Epistle to I. G., An 42
Eric or Little by Little 61
Escreet, Philip 107
Establishing a Fruit Garden 99
Eton College 50, 53, 61, 77, 119, 123
Everest 118
Evors, C. A. 70, 71, 80, 82
Exmoor 103, 111

Fabian, A. H. 95, 119
Fairseat, Highgate 10
Farnborough 82
Farnham, John 18
Farrar, Dean Frederick William 61
Fearon, D. R. 54, 60
Felsted 9
Felton, Revd William appointed 28; disagreement with Governors 31; offer to resign 30
Finchley 17, 66
Finsbury Park 114
First World War 85–7, 88
Fletcher, Sir Frank 81
Ford, William 52–3, 59
Forum, The 99–100
Foster, Samuel 23
Fox, Allan 132
Fox, Thomas 100, 103–4, 115
Free Grammar School of Sir Roger Cholmeley *see* Highgate School
Friends of Highgate School Society 128–9
Fry, E., QC 66

Gabbitas, Thring & Co. 107
Gardiner, Sir Thomas 20
Garner, Lord 127
Gate House, Highgate 12, pl. 1
Gibbon, Hubert 105, 115
Gilbert, Martin 164–5
Giles, Roy Curtis 123–30, 131, 132; appointment 123; attitude to games 125; character 123; opinion of school 123–4; promotion of building 127; religious concern 123, 130
Giles, Mrs Roy 123
Giles, Thomas 30
Gillman, Revd James 46
Girls' school at Highgate 22

Gladstone, W. E. 55–6
Gladstone, William 56
Godwin, W. 21
Goethe 123
Golston 10
Gomshall 111
Gordon Riots 29
Gordonstoun 99
Gough, Donald 101
Green, John 40, 41–2
Griffith, Charles 48
Grindal, Bishop Edmund 8, 12, 13, 14, 15, 16, 40, 42

Hahn, Kurt 99
Haileybury College 47, 61, 69
Haldane, Richard Burdon 85
Hammerson, Michael 114
Hampstead 55
Hampstead and Highgate Express 70, 132
Handel 117
Harben, Philip 100
Haringey 12, 17, 116
Harrison, Revd William 9
Harrow School 9, 19, 32, 50, 53, 97, 135
Hawkshead 16
Headmasters' Conference 55, 121
Heaton-Ellis, R. T. 94–5
Hennell, Lt.-Col. DSO 69
Henry IV, Part I 118
Henry VIII 9, 16
Hetherington, Lt. 70
Hetherington, Sir Roger 107
Hewett, Sir William 14
High Barnet 66
Highgate Ho! 112
Highgate School Archaeological Society 103, 111; assistant masters 62; Consultative Assembly 111, 114; Corps (OTC, JTC) 68–70, 82, 85–6, 92, 102, 105; curriculum 16–17, 26–7, 35, 39, 44, 49, 54, 82–3, 87; Debating Society 66; Dramatic Society 112; Duke of Edinburgh Award Scheme 103, 118; evacuation 101–6; examination, annual 47–8, 49; fees 45; five-day week 126–7; food 80, 86–7; foundation 9–18; foundation scholars 64; future 136; games 50, 51, 67–8, 71–3, 79, 85, 94–5, 96, 97, 98, 118–19, 124 pl. 7; independent magazines 99–100; inspection 35–9; Junior School 64, 82, 93, 100, 101, 106, 132, 133; lawsuit concerning 39–44; Lecture Society 67; Leonardo Society 99; Masaryk Society 111; Mission 77–8; Modelling Club 99; Modern Language Club 99; modern subjects/side 49, 61, 74; music 116–17 Natural History Society 66; numbers 45, 46–7, 62, 71,

Highgate School cont.
75, 80, 81–2, 107–8, 109, 122, 129, 134; parents 55; Pioneers 99; Political Club 99; Pre-Preparatory School 133, 134; quatercentenary 119, 120; removal to Hampstead Lane 51–3; scholarships to universities 47–8; Science Society 67; science teaching 61, 62, 63–4; Scouts 99; Shakespeare Reading Society 67; Sixth Form Council 114; statutes 11–12, 16–17, 19, 22, 40, 45, 64, 135–6; Taunton Commission 53–4; tercentenary 54; uniform 82, 114; Usher 21, 43; V-1 bomb 109, 110

Highgate School (buildings) almshouses 20, 22, 23, 25, 26; Bell-gate 2, 62; Bellevue 102; Buckleigh Place 102; Big School 49–50, 57, 58, 74, 77, 100, 115, 117, 119, 121; Bishop Sandys House 82; British School 63–4; Central Hall 74–5, 87, 88, pl.6; Cerrig Pryfaid 118; chapels 8, 9, 12–15, 17, 19, 23, 24–5, 33, 37, 40, 42–3, 45, 56–7, 58, 57, 87, 126, pl.1, 2; Cholmeley House (Bishopswood Road) 100, 108; Cholmeley House (Southwood Lane) 49, 64, 70, 100, 107, 109, 122; Cordell House 82, 126; Dining Hall 120; Drill Hall 89; Dungeons 74, 100; Dyne House 70, 74, 117, 121, 127, 129; Elgin House 52, 57, 71; Field House 82, 106, 107, 133; Fitzroy Lodge (The Lodge) 52, 71, 105, 132; Garner Building 127, 128; Grindal House 82, 101, 108, 132, 133; Grove Bank 52, 57, 67, 71; Hartland Abbey 101, 106; Jeudwine Library 100; Mallinson Sports Centre 128, 132; Mansfield House 82; Memorial gates 111, pl.8; Northfield Hall 64, 69, 127; Richards Music Centre 132; Sanatorium 64, 127; Schoolhouse/room 9, 15, 17, 33, 37, 38–9, 40, pl. 5; School House 64, 71, 78, 80, 108, 122, 132; Science Building 87–91, 107, 127; Shakespeare Steps 111; Sunshine Café 103, 103; Swimming pool, covered 120, 127; Tabernacle 125, 127; Torridge House 102; Twose's Garage 102; Undercroft 133
Highgate Village 9, 11, 14, 19, 20, 24, 32, 33, 35, 52, 55, 57, 115, 122, pl. 3; Committee of residents 40; fire engine 25–6; pamphleteers 39–42; Robbers Fund 25–6; traffic scheme 119–120

Hill, Jonathan 134
Hitler, Adolf 101
HMS *President IV* 107
Hoare, Sir Samuel 88–9
Hodges, Richard 14
Holloway 48

Homer 48
Hopkins, Gerard Manley 47, 48, 58–9
Hornsey 12, pl. 4
Hornsey Churches Housing Association 22
Horsham 101
Horton, Revd Thomas 24–5, 26
Hosford, Dr Reginald 84, 86, 92, 95, 96, 98
Hunt, Revd Kenneth 93, 95

I. G. *see* Green, John
Ilfracombe 101
Illustrated Sporting and Dramatic News 102–3
Inner Temple 27
Ireton, Gen. Henry 20
Ireton, Sir John 20–1
Isherwood, Robert 38, 39, 40
Islington 12, 39
Izard, Alfred 92

Jeudwine, Edward John Williams 100, 102
Johannesburg 81
Johnston, John Alexander Hope 81–98, 118, 121, 127, 135; appointed 81; changes to curriculum 82–3; character and appearance 83–4, 95–6; disliked by staff 95–6; hissing incident 84–5; promotion of maths and science 81; promotion of technology 87–91; reports to Governors 87–91, 97–98; reorganisation of day-boy houses 82; salary 96; sex education 91–2
Johnston, Mrs John 84, 97
Jones, Miss 51
Julius Caesar 112

Kali, Mr 107
Kay, Walter 71, 73, 74, 79–80, 83
Keble, John 46
Kelly, Edward 94–5
Kennedy, Richard Paul 131–6; character and career 131; concern with academic standards 134; introduction of Deputy Head Master 131; opinion of school 131; promotion of building 132; publicist 131–2
Kent 18
Kentish Town 12, 17
Kenwood House 29, 30
Kenyon, Lord 32
Kinderley, George 47
King, Robert 21
King Lear 67
King's College, Cambridge 67
King's College School, Wimbledon 108
King's School, Canterbury 17, 35, 46, 55
Kingsley, Revd Charles 101
Kinnock, Neil 134
Kipling, Rudyard 102

Kipping, Sidney 109
Kitchener, Field Marshal 87
Knight, Albert 97, 106–7

Lamb, J. G. 69, 70, 71
Lawner, H. J. 66
Leach, C. P. 75
Leech, Revd John Henry 53
Lehmann, R. C. 78
Lincoln's Inn 10, 18
Lindsay, Donald D. 92
Lindstrom, Michael 125
Liptrott, Revd Bexworth 26–7, 28
Lloyd Webber, Andrew 117
London 12, 14, 135
London, Bishop of 9, 12, 13, 18, 22, 28?, 29, 40–1, 64
London, University of 98
Lowe, Douglas G. A. 97, 98
Lucas, N. B. C. 96
Ludgate Hill 31
Lushington, Franklyn 70, 92
Luxmoore, Charles 58–9

McDowall, Dr Charles 61–70, 77; abolition of Rugby football 68; appearance 61; appointment 61; death 70, 71; encouragement of societies 66–7; foundation of Corps 68–70; introduction of modern subjects 61–4; School House opened 64
MacGregor, John 132
Madras system 40
Major, John 134
Mallinson, Theodore 70, 102, 103, 110, 114, 128, 129
Malvern 61
Mansfield, First Earl of 28–32, 33
Mansfield, Third Earl of 42
Marlborough College 46, 47, 49, 51, 61, 62, 77, 91, 101, 109
Marples, Ernest 119
Marriott, Charles 79
Marten, Sir Roger 14
Martin, sexton 36–7, 40
Mary, Queen 9, 10, 12, 14, 17
Masaryk, Jan 111
Masaryk, Thomas 111
Masefield, John 116
Matthews, Susannah 26
Mayo, Revd Charles 34
Mence, Revd Samuel appointment 35; duties as Highgate's parson 38; in court 42–3; interviewed 35–8; later years 45; salary 37–8
Menuhin, Yehudi 116, 121
Merchant of Venice, The 67
Merchant Taylors' 9, 18, 54, 68
Messiah 117
Middlesex 128

Midhurst Grammar School 96
Mill Hill School 109
Mills, Henry 81
Milton, John 93
Mitchinson, Bishop John 55
Molesworth, Capt. 101
Molz, Frederick 83–4, 86, 92, 95
Morning Chronicle 44
Morris, Revd R. L. 60
Moyer, Lady Rebecca 23
Much Ado about Nothing 67
Munche, Dr 49
Munich 101
Murray, William *see* Mansfield, First Earl of

Napoleon 92
Napoleonic Wars 33
National Provincial Bank 106
Newman, Cardinal John Henry 46
New Zealand 128
Nicholl, Sir John 34
Nicholls, Mary 23
No Easy Hopes or Lies 104
Norden, John 12

Odyssey 48
Old Cholmeleian Club/Society 70, 86
Overland Route, The 67
Owen, Dr Henry Butts 39, 40, 42–44
Oxford University 98, 104

Palmer, Alan 104–5
Parliamentary Commission on the Education of the Poor 35–9, 40
Parsifal 117
Pauncefort, Edward 22, 24
Pears, Peter 116
Perks, Charles 76–7
Pevsner, Nikolaus 106
Perth 129
Phelippe, William 12
Pierce, Robert 21
Pitt, William, Earl of Chatham 29
Platt, Williams 19–20, 24
Plowman, Sir Anthony 86, 94
Ponto, The 100
Porter, Revd William 32
Portsmouth 106
Price, Ellis 21
Priestley, J. B. 112
Procktor, Patrick 112
Puleston, Roger 18

Queen's College, The, Oxford 26, 28

Raikes, Robert 32
Rawson, Lionel 76
Raymond, Ernest 116
Read, Robert 122, 124, 126
Repton School 99

INDEX

Resurrection Pie, A 99–100
Richards, David 132
Richardson, A. J. 59
Ringwood 67
Robins, R. W. V. 96, 97, 98, 119
Rossall School 49, 61
Rowe, Nicholas 21
Roy, E. L. 60, 66
Royal Agricultural College, Cirencester 81
Royal Institution 61
Rugby School 9, 32, 46, 50, 53
Rule of St Benedict 123
Russell, Revd John 47
Rutter, John 117, 132

St Bees 12, 109
St Edmund Hall, Oxford 28
St Michael's Church 45, 46, 52, 56, 110
St Michael's School 22
St Pancras 12–13, 19, 34
St Paul's School, 54, 58, 74, 134
Sanders, Revd Ernest 77
Sandys, Bishop Edwin 15, 16, 17
Sawyer, Revd H. A. P. 70
Schoedelin, E. T. 80, 92, 93
School for Scandal 67
Schoppens, Mr 23
Scillies 21
Second World War 101–10
Shah, Sushil 130
Shakespeare 21, 92
Shelley, Howard 117
Shepherd, G. S. pl. 2
She Stoops to Conquer 112
Shrewsbury School 46, 53, 61
Shropshire 18
Simon of Heygate 14
Simons, Revd Sandford B. 70, 77, 93
Skeat, Revd Walter 48–9
Smithfield Market 33
Smythe, Edward 18
Snowdon 118
Society for the Promotion of Christian Knowledge 32
Sodger 50
Solomon 116

Some Account of the Grammar School of Highgate 41
Somerset 18, 26
Somersett, James 29
Somme, Battle of the 87
South Africa 128
Spaniards Inn 30
Spears, Brian 124
Spong, Donald 123
Stalky & Co. 102
Stanford 52
Stewart, Michael 121
Stone, Revd Peter 123
Storer, Edward 27–8
Suez crisis 114
Sylvanus, Harold 92
Symonds, Warden of Wadham 46

Tatham, E. H. R. 66
Tatham, Francis 66
Tatham, John Lawrence 59
Taunton Commission 53–5
Tavener, John 117
Taylor, Philip 71, 73, 79, 80
Taylor, Tom 67
Tchaikovsky 116
Thatcher, Margaret 111
Thomas, John Llewelyn 92
Thring, Edward 46, 55
Throckmorton, Sir Nicholas 10
Times, The 70, 81, 114, 119
Trent College 99
Trinity College, Cambridge 34
Trinity College, Oxford 21, 35
Tom Brown's Schooldays 50
Tonbridge School 81, 95
Totnes 101
Totteridge 66
Tower of London 10, 20
Twidell, Thomas 96, 104, 106–7, 112, 114

University College School 108, 124
Uppingham School 9, 46, 55, 113

Verdi 117
Verdon-Roe, Alliot 91

Vials barber's shop 28
Victoria, Queen 45
Vienna 107
Voice of Highgate 119

Wadham College, Oxford 46, 48
Wales, Prince of (Edward VIII) 91
Walker, C. R. 79
Wallwork, H. C. 101
Walterkyn, Thomas 13
War Requiem 17
Watchman, pamphleteer 39
Waters, R. E. 48
Watford, Charles 92
Waugh, Alec 106
Waugh, Arthur 106–7
Waugh, Evelyn 106
Webb, J. K. G. 119
Wellington College 47, 61, 71
Westminster Abbey 21
Westminster School 29, 32, 50, 54, 126
Westward Ho! 101–6, 107, 116, 129
White, Arthur Preston 103, 104
White, Gilbert 66
Whitechapel 77
Who's Who 71
Wood, W. G. 60, 79, 116
Woods, Francis Cunningham 78, 79, 80, 116
Wollaston, Sir John 20, 22, 24
Worsley, Philip 48
Wigdor, Lucien 91
Wilberforce, Bishop 111
Wilkinson, Sergeant J. 90–1
Williams, John Kyffin 110, 112, 118
Williams, Joshua 19
Williamson, Alexander 86
Williamson, David 126
Winchester College 50, 53, 61, 77
Wyatt, Sir Thomas 10, 28

Yardley, Edward 25
Yates, Edmund 49, 58
York 18
York, Archbishop of 32

Woodman Inn & Post Office
Dorothy Cot.
Wells
Jackson's Lane
Oak Lodge
Convent
The Travellers Inn
York Buildings
NATIONAL SCHOOL
Allotment Gardens
HIGH STREET
Southwood La.
BAPTIST CHAPEL
York Place
South Grove
South Hill Cottages
CEMETERY
Public Footpath
Footpath
Millfield Lane
Stables
Dufferin Lodge
West Hill Lodge
Carlton House
Holly Lodge
Bromwich Walk
Swains Lane
St. Albans Inn
Church Lane
Driftway
Sir T. M. Wilson's Private Road
HAMPSTEAD PONDS
Traitors' or Parliament Hill
Engine House
Steps
HAMPSTEAD JUNCTION RAILW
DARTMOUTH PARK
Building